Laugh? I Nearly To Miami!

A Comedy

Miles Tredinnick

Samuel French – London
New York – Sydney – Toronto – Hollywood

FOR AMATEUR PRODUCTION ENQUIRIES

UNITED KINGDOM AND WORLD EXCLUDING NORTH AMERICA
plays@SamuelFrench-London.co.uk
020 7255 4302/01

Each title is subject to availability from Samuel French,

depending upon country of performance.

LAUGH? I NEARLY WENT TO MIAMI!

First presented by Comedy Hall Productions at the Pentameters Theatre, Hampstead on the 7th June 1985 with the following cast of characters:

Tom Weals	Russell Wootton
Alice Martin	Jill Greenacre
Barney Weals	David Bradshawe
Muriel	Andrea Gordon
Auntie	Gillian Vickers
Frankie	John Lyne-Pirkis
Inspector Hendy	Christopher Prior

The play directed by Charles Harris
Designed by Rik Carmichael

The action of the play takes place in Tom Weals' flat somewhere in Essex

ACT I   One early evening in October
ACT II   The same evening. The action is continuous

Time—the present

A licence issued by Samuel French Ltd to perform this play does not include permission to use any Overture or incidental music specified in this copy. Where the place of performance is already licensed by the Performing Right Society a return of the music used must be made to them. If the place of performance is not so licensed then application should be made to the Performing Right Society, 29 Berners Street, London W1.

A separate and additional Licence from Phonographic Performances Ltd, Ganton House, Ganton Street, London W1 is needed whenever commercial recordings are used.

ACT I*

Tom Weals' first-floor flat in an Essex suburb. It is a foggy evening in October at about 7.30 p.m.

UL is a door leading to the 1st bedroom with a window beside it. Centre is the front door, centre R is the kitchen door. All three doors open on to a carpeted step. There is a small serving hatch, complete with doors, coming from the kitchen, and then there is the bathroom (off R). The 2nd bedroom door is found DR

The flat is sparsely furnished and is obviously more functional than decorative. A slightly shabby three-piece suite stands in the middle of the room with a low coffee table in front of it. A large drinks cabinet with a sliding door is situated underneath the serving hatch. This must be clearly visible to the audience throughout the play. A large desk is placed DL. It has a telephone and a large electric fan on it. Other furniture and fittings include an old-style B/W television set on a small table DR. There are quite a few shelves in the bathroom corner of the room. These are packed solid with Elvis Presley memorabilia, little guitars, badges, magazines, cassettes, calendars, record sleeves. Tom Weals is obviously an Elvis Presley fanatic

As the audience are taking their seats, Elvis Presley songs should be continuously playing in the theatre. As the Lights fade, so does the last song although it can still be heard playing quietly on Tom Weals' portable cassette player when he comes onstage

When the CURTAIN rises the room is empty and the lights are out. Tom and Alice can be heard off outside their front door in the hallway

Tom (*off*) I haven't got the keys, Alice.
Alice (*off*) You have. I gave them to you.
Tom (*off*) And I gave them back. No I didn't, here they are.
Alice (*off*) Told you so.

A key is turned in the lock of the front door and Tom Weals enters his flat. He turns off his cassette player and turns on the main lights. He is forty, good-looking and dressed casually in an Elvis Presley bomber jacket. The most notable feature about him is his hair. He brushes it into a fine quiff at the front like early Elvis Presley. He carries a matching suitcase and a cabin

---

*N.B. Paragraph 3 on page ii of this Acting Edition regarding photocopying and video-recording should be carefully read.

bag which he puts on the coffee table. He then makes straight for the drinks cabinet. He is not in a very good mood

Tom (*angrily*) Of all the things to bloody happen!

Alice Martin, Tom's fiancée stands at the front door. She is in her thirties and very attractive. She is full of fun and life which compares greatly to Tom, who is far more serious and cautious by nature

Alice Tom . . .

Tom (*opening the drinks cabinet and pouring a large Cinzano*) Sometimes I can't believe how bad my luck is.

Alice (*still at the front door*) Oh Tom.

Tom If it had been anyone else, it would have gone like a dream. But not me! Oh no! (*He knocks the drink back in one go*) Not for Tom Weals!

Alice Is Mr Tom Weals going to carry Mrs Tom Weals over the threshold?

Tom We're not married yet.

Alice I know. But we should be. (*She looks at her watch*) About half an hour ago. (*She enters the room and closes the front door*)

Tom A twelve-hour delay! Can you believe it? Twelve sodding hours at the airport!

Alice It was better than yesterday, darling. Yesterday we were there for sixteen hours. I watched the floor polisher change shift twice. (*She places her matching suitcase on the coffee table*)

Tom I still can't believe it. (*He pours another large Cinzano*)

Alice It was the fog, darling. It wouldn't lift.

Tom Fog! It makes me mad that the most important day in our life can be ruined by fog.

Alice That wouldn't lift. (*She takes off her coat*)

Tom We should have flown from Heathrow. Not the local airport.

Alice It was cheaper this way, dear.

Tom We should have paid the extra. It would have been worth it. It's pathetic that our plane should be grounded by fog. They can land men on the moon and blow up the world, surely they can take off through fog? (*He takes off his jacket*)

Alice brushes her hair in an imaginary fourth-wall mirror C. *This is used at various times by all the cast*

Alice Not at our airport, darling.

Tom What's so special about our airport?

Alice It's not all that big. It doesn't have the equipment to deal with fog that refuses to lift.

Tom You're an expert on radar, are you?

Alice No, I was discussing it with the check-in girl.

Tom I suppose that was something to be thankful for. At least we got checked in this time. Our flight actually got called.

Alice (*optimistically*) One step nearer each day.

Tom Very funny.

Alice Tomorrow we'll take off for Miami. (*Wildly*) And then sunshine and sea and ... sand. You'll soon forget about the fog.

Tom (*unconvinced*) I doubt it. It'll probably be here when we get back. We'll be circling for two days trying to land.

Alice Now stop that, Tom. Let's not spoil your lovely romantic idea of getting married and honeymooning in Florida. This time tomorrow we'll be there.

Tom If the flight isn't cancelled again.

Alice Don't be so gloomy, Tom. There's still a tiny chance we might go tonight.

Tom Is there?

Alice The airline said they'd phone if there was a change in the weather.

Alice goes into the kitchen

Tom (*looking out of the window*) Fat chance!

Alice (*off*) Don't worry Tom, we'll soon be there.

Tom (*sitting down on the settee*) It's not just our wedding, Alice. What about the Elvis Presley Convention? We'll have missed the first night.

Alice enters from the kitchen waving a washing-up brush

Alice (*angrily*) Oh damn your Convention!

Tom Alice!

Alice Surely our marriage is more important?

Tom I have been waiting seven years, darling.

Alice So have I!

Tom Not to marry you. I've waited seven years to attend the Convention. Seven years of loyalty to the King and then all this fog. I think I'll sue that TV weatherman. He said it was going to be sunny.

Alice That was a satellite picture of Spain.

Tom Who cares what the weather's like in Spain? Except the Spanish, and they live there so they already know. It's missing the Convention that's really bugging me.

Alice Sometimes I wonder what's more important? Your stupid Convention or our marriage?

Tom (*reassuringly*) Darling, our marriage of course. That's more important than anything.

Alice (*unconvinced*) Really?

Tom Of course.

Alice You do mean that, don't you, Tom?

Tom You know I love you more than anything else.

Alice And I love you too, darling.

Alice sits down beside him on the settee. They kiss each other

Tom Naturally the two were meant to go together. We were to be married at the Convention remember? (*He smiles*) Five hundred Elvis grooms and five hundred Elvis brides walking down the aisle. Can you imagine it? The air thick with the smell of Brylcreem as the choir sing "Are You Lonesome Tonight?"

Alice Not exactly the best choice of song.

Tom I don't know. They might be singing "There Goes My Everything".

Alice I wouldn't mind so much if I was an Elvis fan myself.

Tom (*patiently*) You will be one day, dear. It's a growing appreciation. You can't expect to be crazy about him straight away. It even took me a little while before I got into Elvis. I was a big Pearl Carr and Teddy Johnson fan. (*After a pause*) And then I saw the light.

Alice Sometimes I wonder if it didn't blind you. Your Elvis fanaticism seems to go too far. You make it more important than anything.

Tom I don't. Not everything.

Alice You do.

Tom It's just that Elvis is the King.

Alice *Was* the King. He's dead now.

Tom I know he is *now*. None of us live forever. It's just his memory that carries on. This Convention is the biggest yet, Alice.

Alice The fact remains that he is dead, Tom.

Tom He's still alive to millions of us. I just like to think that I am one of his humble servants. Keeping alive the memory of his name. Nothing wrong in that.

Alice You go too far. You know you do.

Tom Rubbish!

He quite unconsciously runs his hand over his head and pulls off an "Elvis" quiff hairpiece revealing his real hair underneath. It must be a regular occurrence for Alice does not bat an eyelid

Alice I suppose I'd better go and make up the bed in your spare bedroom. (*She stands up and starts for the 2nd bedroom*)

Tom There's no need for that dear.

Alice (*stopping at the door*) I'm afraid I'm an old-fashioned girl Tom. Tomorrow night we can fight over which side of the bed to sleep, tonight I'm still a single girl.

Tom Tomorrow night I was hoping to watch the Japanese dubbed version of "G I Blues".

Alice (*totally put out*) Oh really !!!

Alice exits to the 2nd bedroom

The telephone rings. Tom answers it

Tom (*on the phone*) Hello? ... Who? ... Aunt Mary—how are you? ... It's me. ... Tom ... Tom Weals. ... Alice's fiancé. ... That's right. ... I'll just get her for you. ... Hang on. (*He holds his hand over the phone and shouts*) Alice! It's your auntie!

Alice (*off*) Coming.

Tom (*politely into the phone*) She's just coming, Auntie.

Alice enters from the 2nd bedroom

Tom hands over the phone

Alice (*on the phone*) Hello Auntie. ... I know—but the fog wouldn't lift. ...

Never mind, we should be there tomorrow, fingers crossed. . . . You want to what? . . . (*She looks at Tom, excited*) That would be lovely, Auntie. . . . Very generous indeed. . . . Thank you. . . . Well, any time tonight. . . . That's right, number eleven. . . .

Tom raises his eyes to the ceiling

Look forward to seeing you. . . . Bye-bye, Auntie. (*She replaces the phone*)
Tom (*irritated*) She's not coming around here, is she?
Alice Just for a little while. She only lives around the corner.
Tom Damn that fog! Your Aunt Mary is the last person I want to see.
Alice You've never met her. She might be the most wonderful person in the world.
Tom I feel as if I know her intimately. Your flat is full of her letters. She never lets a week go by. I can spot her handwriting at forty paces.
Alice What's wrong with that? I think she's very sweet. And when she comes around here, I want you on your best behaviour.
Tom Why does she want to come here? Why doesn't she just write?
Alice If you knew the reason, you would not be moaning.
Tom (*starting for the kitchen door*) I don't care what the reason is. I want to spend tonight praying that the fog will lift tomorrow.
Alice I think you'll change your mind.
Tom (*stopping at the kitchen door*) Why? Can she make the sun shine?
Alice She's coming round with our wedding present.
Tom Maybe it's a toaster and she can "pop" off back to where she came from. (*As he goes into the kitchen*) I'm going to make some coffee.

Tom exits to the kitchen

Alice It won't be a toaster. It will be a lot of money.
Tom (*poking his head through the serving hatch*) Money?
Alice I thought that would strike a note.
Tom How much money?
Alice A lot.

Tom comes back into the room

Tom How do you know?
Alice Because that is her style. Auntie is very rich and I'm her favourite niece.
Tom (*most interested*) Are you?
Alice When my cousin George got married, Auntie gave him ten thousand pounds.
Tom (*whistling*) Ten thousand quid! That's a lot of money.
Alice I know. And cousin George wasn't her favourite niece.
Tom Maybe he should've worn a dress.
Alice I'm sure she would've noticed.
Tom Are you sure she's got any money left after playing Father Christmas at all these family weddings?
Alice She's loaded, Tom. So you be nice to her.
Tom Of course I will. (*He smiles*) She's my favourite aunt, after all.

Tom goes into the kitchen

Alice She's very kind. Always giving things to charity.

Tom enters from the kitchen

Tom (*angrily*) We are *not* charity.

Alice We're not exactly rolling in money, darling. Any contribution is welcome. If it wasn't for my part-time job at the Children's Nursery we'd be stuck. And that might disappear with the latest cuts.

Tom You make it sound like we're poor.

Alice How would you like to make it sound then?

Tom We're just going through a tough period. Everyone is. I'm taking you on a lovely honeymoon to Florida. How many couples can say that?

Alice I know, darling. But it did take you five years saving up for it.

Tom That's not true. (*After a pause*) It was more like eight.

Alice I'm not saying that you haven't got a good job. Working at that grocer's at least means we won't starve.

Tom It's not a grocer's! It's a delicatessen.

Alice Call it what you like. I just wish they would pay you more. After all, your customers are rich and they spend a lot of money.

Tom We're getting a raise next year. Hopefully.

Alice Well, when Auntie comes, try and look slightly impoverished. We want to win her sympathy.

Tom (*sarcastically*) That shouldn't be too difficult. I'm just a penniless delicatessen assistant. If it wasn't for the occasional theft of a tin of "crabs in honey", I would have starved to death ages ago.

Alice Don't get childish, Tom. (*Starting for the 2nd bedroom door*) Now I had better go and get that bed made.

Alice exits into the bedroom

Tom I'm going to blend some coffee beans.

Tom starts for the kitchen. The doorbell rings. It's an "Elvis" doorchime that plays "Return to Sender" or any other Elvis song

Oh blast, she's here already. (*Calling out*) Alice, your auntie's arrived.

There's no reply from Alice so Tom makes for the door himself. The doorbell rings again

All right, all right. Keep your hair on.

Tom puts his wig on and quiffs it up in the fourth-wall mirror. He is just about to unlock the front door when it opens

Barney Weals, Tom's brother enters. He is a good-looking man-about-town in his thirties and wears a fashionable suit with open-necked shirt. He is as shocked to see Tom, as Tom is to see him

Barney!

Barney Tom! What are you doing here?

Tom I live here. How did you get in?

Barney You gave me your spare key. (*He puts the key on the coffee table*)

Tom Then why are you ringing the bell?

Barney To make sure it works. I've got a girl coming here tonight who makes Hot Gossip look like idle chit-chat. But I won't even get warm if your doorbell is broken. (*He moves to the drinks cabinet, opens it and checks the supply*)

Tom I got it fixed last week. What's all this about a girl? And what are you doing with my booze?

Barney I'm just making sure that there is enough for your brother to be able to make his killer cocktail—(*with a wink*)—"Barney's Leg-Openers!"

Tom And what's that?

Barney A little bit of everything you've got in here. (*He searches through the cabinet*)

Tom She'll be as sick as a parrot in the morning.

Barney As long as she's as wild as a monkey tonight, who cares? She is a cracker Tom, and I intend to pull her.

Tom I'm pleased to hear it, but what is she doing coming here?

Barney You lent me the flat, remember?

Tom (*looking blank*) Did I?

Barney All week. For me to do as I please. And tonight that's what I intend to do. (*He takes a small bowl and a bag of peanuts from his jacket pocket. He empties peanuts into the bowl and places it on the coffee table. He takes a candle and holder out of the other pocket and also places it on the coffee table*)

Tom You can't.

Barney You promised me, Tom. You said you wanted someone around to keep an eye on things. Make sure you wouldn't get burgled. (*He looks around the room*) Not that you've got anything worth stealing.

Tom I'm afraid it's out of the question tonight, Barney.

Tom picks up the bowl of peanuts and empties them into Barney's right-hand jacket pocket along with the candle and holder. Some of the nuts fall on to the settee

Barney Why? (*He looks at Tom hard*) Something has just struck me, Tom.

Tom What?

Barney Shouldn't you be in Miami?

Tom Yes, I——

Barney Getting married to Alice? (*He moves over to Tom*)

Tom Yes, but the——

Barney And honeymooning amongst alligators and Bermuda pants?

Tom I should be. Yes.

Barney (*putting his arm around Tom*) My poor old brother. I'm so sorry. What happened? Did she call it off? Break the engagement?

Tom It was the——

Barney You can tell me, Tom. I'm family. You can let it all out with me. Let the tears roll.

Tom (*removing Barney's arm*) There's nothing to cry about. The flight has been cancelled, that's all. Beyond our control. We're now going as soon as they phone us. Probably tomorrow.

Barney I see. (*He sits down in the chair*)

Tom So I'm afraid your seduction will have to take place elsewhere.

Barney Impossible. She's coming here at eight.

Tom Then you'll have to get in touch with her. Call it off.

Barney I can't.

Tom Why not? Just pick up the phone.

Barney She's a telephonist on Directory Enquiries. I can never get through.

Tom You'll have to do something.

Barney (*inspired*) You've got a spare bedroom. (*He stands up and moves to the 2nd bedroom door*) We'll go in there. We won't disturb you.

Tom throws himself in the way

Tom You can't. It's being used by Alice.

Barney By Alice?

Tom We're not married yet, Barney. Alice is an old-fashioned girl in these things.

Barney Is she really?

Tom So you'll just have to wait downstairs until your girlfriend arrives and then I'm afraid it's back to your place.

Barney I can't do that.

Tom Why ever not?

Barney I've let my flat out to my bookie. For him and his Girl Friday. And they won't be out till Monday.

Tom God! It's like "Heartbreak Hotel"!

Barney It helps me pay the rent, Tom. Things aren't that easy when you've got no money.

Tom Why don't you get yourself a respectable job?

Barney If I was working I wouldn't have time to look after my other interests. You've got to have irons in fires, you know.

Barney checks his appearance in the fourth-wall mirror and is impressed with his reflection. Tom stands behind him jockeying for position and attends to his quiff

Tom Yes, well be a blacksmith somewhere else. (*He moves to the front door*) I've got enough on my plate without your housing problems.

Barney Call yourself a brother? I don't know why I can't just use your spare bedroom. (*He sits down on the couch and puts his feet up on the coffee table*)

Tom I've told you. It's already occupied.

Barney You're so unadventurous, Tom. Why don't you insist she sleeps with you? Crack the whip so to speak.

Tom I will, when we're married.

Barney Hell! Can't you break with convention now and again?

Tom It's not me, Barney. I have to respect Alice's feelings.

Barney You never had any spirit, did you?

Tom What do you mean?

Barney Remember that time Dad asked us what we would like to do if we had the choice of anything in the world?

Tom Vaguely.

Barney I said I wanted to rob a bank and be the richest man in the world.

Tom Typical.

Barney And you said you wanted to win a cooking badge in the Scouts.

Tom So what?

Barney It says a lot about our characters.

Tom All it shows is that I'm honest and you're not.

Barney Rubbish! I've just got more get up and go!

Tom Yes, well why don't you get up and go? (*He lifts Barney's feet off the coffee table*)

Barney (*standing up*) You never take risks, do you?

Tom I've done some pretty daring things in my time. You'd be surprised.

Barney Like what? No television licence? (*He points at the TV set and moves to the front door*)

Tom I'll tell you sometime when I'm not so busy. Now if you don't mind . . . ? (*He opens the front door*)

Barney All right, but I don't call this brotherly love. I'll wait for Muriel downstairs.

Tom She's actually got a name then? Not just a number in your filing system?

Barney Ha ha, Tom. Her name is Muriel.

Tom I never did approve of the way you keep records of your bed partners.

Barney At least I've got some bed partners.

Tom And don't bring them around here until I've gone to Miami. Alice hates you enough as it is. Make sure we've moved out before you move in.

Barney Don't forget to send me a postcard. You know the address.

He exits briskly out of the front door

Tom Randy bugger! (*He closes the front door and removes his quiff*)

The 2nd bedroom door opens and Alice enters

Alice That's got the bed made, now I've got to unpack my case.

Tom Hardly worth doing, dear. You'll only have to pack it again in the morning.

Alice I can only sleep in my nightdress. Otherwise I get bad dreams that I'm being chased across fields by crazy Vikings!

Tom (*concerned*) Oh darling, I didn't know.

Alice Haven't I told you dear? The Vikings get nearer and nearer with their knives and their lustful eyes. And then after the worst bit I wake up in a terrible sweat.

Tom What's the worst bit?

Alice You turn up and rescue me!

Tom reacts but does not answer

Who were you talking to?

Tom That was a wrong number.

Alice A wrong number? There was someone in here. I heard voices.

Tom When I say wrong number, I mean they were looking for number twelve and we're number eleven.

Alice I know this is number eleven, Tom. It says so on the door. How could anyone be confused? Number twelve is next door. Where there is a big twelve.

Tom I know. They just popped in here enquiring about number twelve.

Alice The voice sounded to me like your horrible brother Barney.

Tom (*throwing his hands up in defeat*) Did it?

Alice You know how much I dislike him, Tom. I don't want him hanging around. He's nothing but trouble.

Tom He only popped around for a chat. He's having a few problems with his new girlfriend. He doesn't know where to take her.

Alice What's wrong with the cinema?

Tom That's probably where he'll end up.

Alice That man is a bad influence on you, Tom.

Tom He's not, Alice. I don't listen to his ideas.

Alice What ideas.

Tom The way he thinks about things. His outlook on life.

Alice He hasn't got an outlook. All he thinks about is sex! And when he's not thinking about it, he's having it!

Tom Yes, well I don't listen to him.

Alice I should think not. We're not married yet.

Tom But when all is said and done he is my brother.

Alice Well I don't like him and I certainly don't trust him.

Tom He's got his annoying habits, I know.

Alice (*moving to the coffee table to pick up the case*) Now which of these cases is mine? I knew this matching luggage was a mistake. (*She picks up one of the cases*)

Tom I think you've got the wrong one there, dear. That one is mine.

Alice Nonsense! It's mine. I can tell by the weight. I have been carrying the damn thing for two days.

Tom And I can tell just by *looking* at it, Alice. That case is definitely mine. No doubt about it.

Alice I'm afraid not, dear. (*She grabs the case*) It is mine.

Tom It's not.

Alice It is!

Tom It's mine! Let go of it! (*He grabs the case*)

They struggle over the case pulling it back and forth between each other. The lid flies open and bundles of banknotes cascade out on to the floor

What the hell!!!

Alice What on earth!!!

Tom It's money! Tons of it! (*He doubletakes as he opens and shuts the case quickly*)

Alice What have you done? Robbed a bank?

Tom (*looking inside the case*) Whose is it?

Alice It was in *your* case.

Tom It wasn't. It was in yours. (*He thinks about it*) No, on second thoughts it was in my case.

Alice (*falling down on her knees and flicking through the banknotes*) There must be thousands of dollars here.

Tom How did it get in there? I don't remember putting it in there.

Alice Are you sure?

Tom Of course I'm sure. I put in pyjamas, toothpaste, Brylcreem, socks. I did not put all this money in there. I would have remembered.

Alice What shall we do, Tom?

Tom We'll have to hand it in to the police. We can't keep it. It would be dishonest.

Alice You don't know where this money came from.

Tom Nor do you.

Alice For all you know, it might have been some eccentric millionaire who took pity on you. Slipped it in your case when you weren't looking.

Tom (*incredulous*) Eccentric millionaire? Don't be daft. That sort of thing only happens in Walt Disney films. (*After a pause*) In real life they would probably leave it to a cat home.

Alice (*flicking through the money*) This much money would buy a lot of cat food.

Tom It's my duty to tell the police. (*He lifts the telephone*)

Alice Let me count it first. (*She snatches the receiver and replaces it*)

Tom Why?

Alice We want to know how much it is, don't we?

Tom What does it matter? We're not going to spend it.

Alice The law states that if it is not claimed within four weeks, it returns to the finder.

Tom I think someone is going to notice it's missing and then they'll claim it.

Alice Nevertheless, I want to know exactly how much we've got. (*She starts to pick the bundles up*)

Tom All I want to know is what it's doing in *my* suitcase.

Alice (*spotting a label on the back of the case*) Good God! Look!

Tom What?

Alice The label. Look at the name on the label. It's not yours.

Tom So it is your case.

Alice (*examining the label closely*) It belongs to a Mr Pintocelli.

Tom Who's Mr Pintocelli?

Alice I don't know, but this must be his case.

Tom Do you think he was another passenger on the Miami flight?

Alice (*it clicks*) That's it! He must have been. All the cases were checked in and you must have picked up the wrong ones when the flight was cancelled.

Tom Why is it always my fault?

Alice Because I didn't pick the cases up. You did.

Tom That means this Mr Pintocelli has got my case.

Alice Not necessarily.

They both look at the 2nd case

Unless . . .

Tom Unless that's it.

Alice Open it!

Tom (*opening the case*) Oh no! (*More bundles of money fall on to the floor*) I don't believe it!

Alice More money! (*She throws the notes into the air*) We're rich! We're rich! (*She throws more money into the air*)

Tom runs around desperately trying to catch them

Tom Stop it, Alice! There must be a million here!

Alice We don't know for sure. I'll have to count it.

The doorbell rings. They both panic

Tom Heavens! Who's that! The police! We'll be thrown in jail, Alice! (*Aghast*) I'll get attacked in the showers! Oh my God!

Alice Don't be stupid! How can it be the police?

Tom (*almost hysterical*) I haven't even stolen the bloody money!

Alice Not yet, no.

Tom What do you mean by that?

Alice We'll discuss it later. What shall I do now?

Tom Take the money into the bedroom. Quickly!

Alice quickly stuffs both suitcases with banknotes and moves to the 2nd bedroom door. As she does this she drops bundles of notes on the floor. Tom follows her cramming them into his pockets. The doorbell rings again

Come on for God's sake!

Alice, with the two suitcases, exits into the 2nd bedroom

Tom grabs his quiff and puts in on his head slightly off-centre. He then opens the front door

Barney enters

What the hell do you want now?

Barney I've come back for my key. (*He sees the key on the coffee table and moves towards it*)

Tom That key belongs to me.

Barney You gave it to me. (*He picks up the key off the table*)

Tom Yes, well now I want it back. (*He snatches the key*)

Barney How am I going to get in then? (*He snatches the key back*)

Tom You're not going to get in. (*He snatches the key back*)

Barney We had an agreement, Tom. (*He snatches the key back and holds it just out of Tom's reach*)

Tom I've changed my mind. (*He tries to grab the key*)

Barney Why? What's the reason?

Tom No specific reason. One or two things just turned up out of the blue, that's all.

Barney I bet this is because of Alice.

Tom Nothing to do with her at all.

Barney Whatever the reason, I'm going to keep the key. (*He pockets the key*)

Tom Then I'll change the locks.

Barney You said I could have this place the whole time you were in Miami.

Tom I'm not in bloody Miami!

Barney You will be soon.

Tom I'm going off the idea very quickly.

Barney What? You've been saving up for years. It's cost you a pretty penny. I know that you and Alice don't have that much money.

Tom That's not strictly true.

Tom takes a handkerchief out of his pocket to wipe away nervous sweat from his forehead. A few $50 notes flutter to the ground. Barney, facing the other way, doesn't notice this

Barney I mean, look at this old flat. You're mortgaged up to the hilt and what for?

Tom At least I own something. (*He crawls around on the floor picking up $50 notes. He stuffs them in his pockets*)

Barney (*turning around but unable to see Tom*) You're better off rent—— Tom? Where are you?

Tom (*from the floor*) Down here.

Barney (*moving to Tom*) What are you doing down there?

Tom I've lost some money.

Barney (*pointing at the floor*) There's a twopenny piece you missed there. By your knee.

Tom (*picking up the coin*) Thank you. (*He stands up*)

Barney You must be very hard up, Tom. Worse than I thought.

Tom Not really. But every penny counts.

Barney (*putting his hand in his pocket*) Let me lend you a few quid.

Tom No! No! There's no need.

Barney There's no need to be proud with me, Tom (*He offers him £3*) I may be broke but I am family.

Tom I don't need your money, Barney.

Barney Take it. Just in case.

Tom Believe me, I've got quite enough of my own.

Barney Not if you have to go crawling on the floor picking up coins. (*He holds out the money*) Go on, take it.

Tom (*firmly*) No thank you. I still haven't forgotten about your engagement present.

Barney The silver candlesticks?

Tom That had "Savoy Hotel" engraved on the bottom.

Barney A slight oversight, Tom. It could have happened to anyone.

Tom Your dishonesty doesn't impress me, Barney. You want to be careful. You start small and before long it's violent crime. People doing things up your dark alleyways.

Barney Not me, mate. I'd run a mile from the heavy mobs. A silver candlestick's one thing ...

Tom Just watch it. (*He points at the front door*) Anyway, you'd better get going. If Alice sees you ...

Barney (*starting for the front door*) Only if you say I can use your flat when you've gone.

Tom Yes, yes anything. Just get out. I've got a few things on my mind.

Barney OK but as soon as you've gone, I'll be your resident security man. (*He holds up the key*)

Tom Just make sure I have gone. I don't want Alice coming back and finding unfamiliar underwear lying around. Especially just after we're married.

Barney Leave it to me, Tom. No "D" cups at breakfast time!

Barney is just about to leave when ...

The 2nd bedroom door opens and Alice comes rushing out. She is very excited

Alice Five hundred thousand Tom, there's five hundred——(*She sees Barney*) Hello Barney.

Barney Hello Alice. (*He moves back to the centre of the room*)

Alice What are ... what are you doing here?

Barney Just dropped by. What's the excitement?

Alice Excitement?

Barney Your five hundred thousand. Have you won the pools or something?

Alice No ... er ... yes.

Barney (*most interested*) Really. You didn't mention it, Tom. What was it? The pools? The gee-gees?

Alice } (*together*) { Pools
Tom } { Gee-gees.

Barney Make your mind up.

Alice } (*together*) { Gee-gees.
Tom } { Pools.

Barney What? On both? How much did you say again?

Alice Er ... five hundred thousand.

Tom Is what we *could* win if we bet on the right horse——

Alice —and it won——

Tom —which of course it hasn't——

Alice —Yet.

Barney You would have to lay out an awful lot of money to win five hundred thousand. (*He takes out a cigarette packet*) Quite frankly, I don't believe you. (*To Tom*) Tell me the truth.

Tom The truth?

Barney About this five hundred thousand.

Tom Well ... er ... I ...

Alice If you must know, it's ... er ... um ... (*She sees Barney light his cigarette*) ... how much we would save altogether if Tom gave up smoking!

Barney (*incredulous*) Five hundred thousand!

Alice (*quickly*) Over fifty years.

Tom But I don't smoke!

Alice But if you did, Tom. Imagine the saving.

Tom I didn't know cigarettes were that expensive.

Barney They're not.

Alice Don't forget the matches and the rate of inflation.

Barney I never thought of it like that. (*He stubs out his cigarette in an ashtray*) There, that must have saved me about a hundred and fifty.

Alice You have to think of these things.

Tom Barney was just leaving. Weren't you, Barney?

Barney Was I?

Alice Why did you come around, Barney?

Barney I ... er ...

Tom He just came around to say that he was sorry we didn't get off to Miami.

Alice Yes, well it's most annoying but we should be there tomorrow.

Barney (*moving to the front door*) I must be off then. Have a good honeymoon. Maybe you'll have won some real money by the time you get back.

Barney exits

Tom (*quickly removing his quiff*) Thank God he's gone. The money? How much did you say?

Alice Five hundred thousand dollars!

Tom Half a million! Are you sure?

Alice Of course I'm sure. I've just counted it. It's mainly in fifty-dollar bills.

Tom What are we going to do with it?

Alice I've had a long think about it.

Tom And?

Alice I think we should keep it.

Tom (*aghast*) We can't!

Alice Why not?

She goes into the 2nd bedroom and reappears with one of the suitcases. She takes out a bundle of money and waves it at Tom

This will set us up for life, Tom. You'll be able to give up your job at the delicatessen, and I can become a cut-back.

Tom I don't want to give up my job.

Alice You'll have to. You'll be richer than most of your customers. We'll be able to move out of here and live in luxury, Tom. We must *keep* the money.

Tom I don't want to live in luxury on someone else's money. I want to live in luxury on my own.

Alice (*exploding*) YOU HAVEN'T GOT ANY MONEY!!!

Tom I'm saving up!

Alice You'll be dead by the time you've saved up this much. This is our one big chance, Tom. Because of a mistake we've got five hundred thousand dollars in cash sitting here. Let's pack it in the cases and take off for Brazil or somewhere.

Tom (*firmly*) Certainly not! We're going to Miami. Don't forget the Elvis Convention.

Alice Bugger the Convention! With this much money you can buy it. Next year you can make them hold it in your garden.

Tom It is tempting, but no ... we must return this money to its rightful owner.

Alice All of it?

Tom All of it. Every penny.

Alice Couldn't we just keep a little back? Say twenty-five thousand dollars?

Tom No we can not! This money does not belong to us, Alice. It belongs to this Mr Pintocelli who at this moment is probably feeling terrible. Imagine he gets home and opens his case to check his money and what does he find? My pyjamas, toothpaste, Brylcreem and socks!

Alice I still think a little wouldn't go amiss.

Tom I wouldn't be able to sleep at night, Alice.

Alice I won't be able to sleep if we give it back!

Tom There must be an address on the label. We'll take the cases back if he lives locally. I'll go and get the other one.

Tom exits into the 2nd bedroom

Alice starts to hide bundles of the money in the drinks cabinet

Alice I think you're being foolish, Tom. Think what we could do with all that money.

Tom (*off*) From inside prison? Forget it, Alice.

Alice hides more bundles in the cabinet

Alice We wouldn't get caught.

Tom enters from the 2nd bedroom carrying the 2nd case

Alice slides the drinks cabinet door shut

Tom Of course we would. This Mr Pintocelli can't be that stupid. He's going to realize he's lost his money straight away. And then he'll see he's got the wrong case and he'll call the police, and they'll be around before you can whistle "Rags to Riches".

Alice With this money you could be rich, Tom.

Tom (*sternly*) We take the money back. (*He looks at the label on the case*) Now where does this Mr Pintocelli live? We're in luck! He's staying at the *Royal Hotel*. It's only down the road. We can nip down there and be back in a matter of minutes.

Alice What happens if he's not there? Can we keep the money then?

Tom If he's not there, we'll see him at the airport tomorrow. I'm going to be totally honest, Alice. When this is all over I'll have a clear conscience.

Alice Why not have a guilty one, on a beach in Brazil?

Tom (*looking at her closely*) I never realized how dishonest you were, Alice. I trust this won't be a regular occurrence.

Alice It's hardly a regular occurrence with half a million dollars landing in our laps, is it?

Tom No, and that is why I refuse to let it change our lives.

Alice Bloody hell!!!

Tom Alice! Language!

Alice Are you going to be this unadventurous all our married life?

Tom Ask me in Miami. After we're married. (*He puts the banknotes into the cases and shuts them*) Honesty is the best virtue, darling.

Alice I am being honest. I want to keep the money.

Tom You'll think differently in the morning. (*He puts on his quiff*)

Alice I won't. I won't feel any different at all.

Tom Come on, Alice. We'll sing a couple of verses of "Promised Land" on the way. (*He puts on his jacket*)

Alice Oh bugger Elvis! (*She grabs her coat*)

Tom Alice . . .

Tom picks up both cases and walks to the front door. Alice follows him. He turns the lights out and they both exit as the door slams shut

There is a moment of silence and then a key is turned in the lock. Barney enters. He turns on the light

Barney This is it, Muriel. Come on in.

Muriel enters. She is an extremely attractive girl in her mid-twenties, with a cockney accent. She wears a coat over a very sexy evening dress and accessories. She is looking forward to a fun evening

Muriel Are you sure this is your flat?

Barney Of course. Otherwise I wouldn't have the key, would I?

Muriel Why did we have to hide in the front porch then? When I go home, I go straight in. I don't hide in the porch. People probably thought we were burglars.

Barney It's like I told you, Muriel. I was waiting for my brother and his er . . . wife to leave. They've been staying here a few days. I didn't want to bump into them.

Muriel Oh, I see.

Barney But now they're going to Miami on their . . . er . . . holidays. You saw the suitcases yourself. (*He takes the candle and holder out of his pocket. The candle is broken. He tries to make it stand up on the coffee table*)

Muriel He seemed in an awful hurry.

Barney They don't want to miss their plane.

Muriel Oh.

Barney So there's nothing to worry about. We've got the whole place to ourselves. Let me take your coat off.

Muriel Ta.

He takes her coat off

Not a bad little place you've got here. You're doing it up, I suppose.

Barney I, er . . . yes. It needs some money put into it of course. To get it up to my standards.

Muriel Why don't you spend some then?

Barney The thing is Muriel that I haven't lived here very long.

Muriel Just moved in, have you? (*She checks her appearance in the fourth-wall mirror*)

Barney No! Yes! Yes, I moved in two days ago as a matter of fact. I haven't got my interior decorator in yet.

Muriel What about your brother?

Barney No good at all. Absolutely hopeless with a paint brush. He'd probably think this is well-decorated. (*He looks around the room*)

Muriel No, I meant the problem.

Barney Problem? What problem?

Muriel Between you and your brother. You said you didn't want to bump into him.

Barney looks blank

That's why we hid in the porch, wasn't it?

Barney Oh yes.

Muriel (*sitting down on the settee*) So what's the lack of brotherly love?

Barney Er . . . jealousy. (*He sits down beside her*)

Muriel Jealousy?

Barney Yes. Pure, driven, unadulterated jealousy.

Muriel Of you? (*She laughs*)

Barney Yes. He's green with envy.

Muriel I can't see why he should be jealous of you.

Barney He's the poor relation you see.

Muriel Hasn't he got much money?

Barney Hasn't got any money.

Muriel And you have?

Barney Let's say I'm comfortably off. (*He strokes her knee*)

Muriel (*looking around the room*) If you say so.

Barney I do.

He leans over to kiss her. She stands up and his head lands in a cushion

Muriel How can he afford to fly to Miami then? If he's so poor?

Barney He's been saving up for years. Anyway, enough about him. It's you and me that matters. (*He pats the empty space beside him*) Why don't you come and sit down?

Muriel I've been sitting down all day. Let's have a dance. Got any records?

Barney stands up, close to her. She feels the bulge in his right pocket

What's that?

Barney They're my nuts, Muriel. (*He pours nuts into the bowl and puts them on the table*)

Muriel walks to the drinks cabinet. He follows

We can dance later on. Afterwards.

Muriel After what?

Barney After a ... after a drink. (*He leans on the drinks cabinet*) You'd like a drink, wouldn't you?

Muriel Yeah, all right. What have you got?

Barney How about one of my cocktails?

Muriel All right, but don't make it too strong. I like to keep in control. So I can enjoy myself. (*She winks at Barney and walks over to the record collection*)

Barney I'll make it medium strength. (*He opens the drinks cabinet and bundles of money fall on to the floor*) Bloody hell!!!

Muriel (*not seeing this*) This "saving up" your brother goes in for. It's a good idea if you ask me. What's he got? A piggy bank?

Barney What? (*He quickly puts the money back into the cabinet and slides the door shut*)

Muriel I keep a piggy bank. I've had one since I was a child.

Barney opens the cabinet again to check he saw what he saw. Satisfied, he slams it shut again

Trouble is I'll have to smash it open to get the coins out. My fingers are too big to get in the hole. (*She pulls out a record*) Oh look! Here's one of Elvis. Of course, if you don't want to save up you can always rob a bank. That's been a fantasy of mine you know. The trouble is if you get the "Mob" after you.

Barney (*horrified*) The "Mob"?

Muriel Yeah, the "Family" chasing you for the money. They're heavy these crime families. Even sweet old Grandma will blow your brains out!!! (*She looks at Barney*) Are you all right, Barney?

Barney (*turning to face her*) What? Yes, yes I'm fine.

Muriel You look a little pale.

Barney I've just stumbled across something quite incredible.

Muriel What? Nothing to drink?

Barney No, no there's plenty to drink.

Muriel Well, let's have one then. I'm parched. You wouldn't believe how thirsty you get saying "What town please?" all day long.

Barney (*moving over to Muriel*) Why don't we go out for a meal somewhere?

Muriel I thought you were going to knock something up here.

Barney I was! I will! I just don't really fancy it now. Let's eat out.

Muriel Make up your mind. I was hoping for a romantic evening for two here.

Barney I know a lovely Italian place just around the corner.

Muriel I don't like foreign food.

Barney Watch me eat it then. I love it.

Muriel (*sarcastically*) You're so full of charm.

Barney (*pointing at the bathroom door*) Now go to the bathroom and powder your nose.

Muriel I don't want to powder my nose!!!

Barney Well find something to do in there. (*He pushes Muriel into the bathroom*)

Muriel exits to the bathroom

(*To himself*) Where did he get all that money? (*He moves to the drinks cabinet, opens it and looks at the money*) He must have robbed a bank! (*Realizing*) Oh my God! The five hundred thousand! He said he'd done something daring. This is it. He's robbed a bank. My own brother. It's always the quiet ones. Always the ones who say they'd rather be getting a cooking badge in the Scouts.

The telephone rings

Who the hell's that? (*He pushes the money back into the drinks cabinet and slams the door shut. He picks up the phone*) Hello? . . . Yes, Mr Weals speaking . . . Oh the money . . . Yes. . . . It's *your* money. . . . Of course you can come and get it. . . . I won't tell a soul mate. . . . If I do, you'll do what? . . . Cut off my . . . ? WHAT! . . . Both of them? You can't cut off both . . . UUUURGH!!! . . . You can't do things like that . . . I promise you no-one else knows about it but me . . . Tom Weals. . . . (*He looks around, gulps nervously*) Of course I'm Tom Weals. . . . Listen, I wouldn't even tell my own brother, mate. . . . You can trust me . . . (*He replaces the receiver*) Bloody hell!!! (*To himself*) He's going to cut off my ears. Both of them! I won't be able to hear myself screaming. What sort of gangsters has Tom got in with? I must hide the money in a safe place and get out of here.

Barney opens the drinks cabinet and picks up a few bundles of banknotes. He then moves to the 2nd bedroom door

Suddenly Muriel enters from the bathroom

Muriel I've powdered my nose Barney.

Barney panics and sticks the money under a cushion on the settee. He then sits on it with his arms folded

Barney Oh good.
Muriel What now?
Barney Why don't you er . . . why don't you take a quick bath?
Muriel A bath! Why should I want a bath? I'm not dirty.
Barney Of course you're not. It's just that this bath is rather special.
Muriel (*unconvinced*) A rather special bath?
Barney Yes. It's er . . . it's very comfortable.
Muriel Comfortable?
Barney Yes, you just lie back in it and totally relax.
Muriel Sounds like any other bath to me.
Barney Yes, but the view is lovely.
Muriel View? Looking at the taps?
Barney Why don't you go and find out for yourself?
Muriel (*angry*) Now look here! I'm getting rather fed up with all this. I came here for a nice night out. I want a laugh, not a bath! So far it's been a disaster.
Barney What do you mean?

Muriel (*counting off on her fingers*) First of all we had to hide in the porch to get in, you haven't given me a drink, you suggest we go and eat something I don't like, you want me to take a bath and at the end of the evening you expect me to hop into bed with you. I've only got one question. Why the hell should I?

Barney (*embarrassed*) I wasn't expecting you to hop into bed with me.

Muriel THEN I AM WASTING MY TIME!!! (*She picks up her coat and moves to the front door*) I'll see you around, Barney.

Barney Wait! Wait a minute. Don't go yet. (*He blocks her way*) It's just that ... well ... it's just that I wasn't expecting you to be so forward.

Muriel I'm a modern girl, Barney. I decide who's going to have me.

Barney Blimey!!! Of course. Look, why don't you go into the kitchen and make some coffee. I just want to make one phone call and then we'll go out and have a lovely meal.

Muriel Somewhere I want to eat?

Barney Anywhere.

Muriel No foreign food?

Barney Fish and chips, anything you like.

Muriel (*moving* c) OK, but let's get on with it. I'm back on shift at eight.

Barney (*opening the kitchen door*) The kitchen's in here.

Muriel exits to the kitchen

Right, the money. (*He takes the bundles of banknotes out from under the cushion and throws them into the drinks cabinet*)

Suddenly Muriel pops out through the serving hatch

Barney slams the cabinet door shut

Muriel Instant or percolated? I see you know your beans.

Barney (*in panic*) Per ... per ... percolated.

Muriel It'll take longer.

Muriel disappears, closing the hatch

Barney No problem. (*To himself*) Right, the airport. Now what's the number? Directory Enquiries. (*He dials 192 on the phone*) I must get in touch with Tom before he gets on that plane. Find out what he wants to do with all this money. He can't leave it here. (*He rattles his fingers*) Why oh why don't they answer? They're so bloody slow. (*An idea strikes him. He replaces the phone and opens the kitchen door*) Operator?

Muriel (*off*) Yeah?

Barney Can I have the number for the airport please?

Muriel (*off, with a posh telephone voice*) Heathrow, Gatwick or the local?

Barney The local.

Muriel (*off*) Arrivals, departures or cargo?

Barney Departures.

Muriel (*off, automatically*) The number you want is four five two two five.

Barney (*closing the door*) Thank you operator. (*He dials the number on the phone*) If I can only catch him before he gets on that plane.

The doorbell rings

Oh my God! (*He replaces the phone*) They're here. This is it, Barney. Brace yourself. Hand over the money and you won't be hearing from them again. Keep the money and you won't be hearing anyone again! I'll see how big they are first. (*He checks his appearance in the fourth-wall mirror and starts for the front door. He then runs back to the mirror and pulls his hair down over his ears*) Coming, coming.

The doorbell rings again. He opens the front door

It is Alice's Auntie carrying a large bag. She is an eccentric figure in her sixties and slightly deaf. She wears a black "Godfather" style hat

Auntie (*jolly*) Hello there. You must be Tom.
Barney (*terrified*) Er ... yes ... I'm ... er ... Tom Weals. How do you do? (*He shakes her hand, keeping his other hand over one of his ears*)
Auntie I know your name is Weals, Tom. Must we be so formal? Please call me Auntie.
Barney (*taken aback at this friendliness*) Right, er Auntie. I suppose you've come about the money.
Auntie All in good time, Tom. Do you mind if I sit down? My legs aren't what they were. (*She moves to the settee*)
Barney (*horrified*) Your legs! What happened to them?
Auntie Sorry? What did you say? I'm a little deaf.
Barney (*putting his hands over his ears*) Oh my God!
Auntie (*sitting down on the settee*) Do sit down, Tom. You make me nervous jumping about. (*She takes off her hat*)
Barney (*instantly obeying*) Anything you say. (*He sits on a chair*)
Auntie (*looking around the room*) Where's my favourite niece then?
Barney (*totally blank*) I don't know. You tell me.
Auntie (*winking at Barney*) Tied up in the kitchen I expect.
Barney What! Your own niece!
Auntie If she doesn't do what you tell her Tom, let me know. I'll soon put her right. She can be a spoilt little madam at times.
Barney I don't even know her!
Auntie Not as well as I do, I'll admit. But after a few years you'll know her inside out. When you're a member of the "Family".
Barney I don't want to know her, thank you, Auntie.
Auntie You want to keep a little mystery about her, do you? Wise man. A little mystery keeps the flames of passion alive.
Barney Look, I'm sure your niece is a marvellous girl but can we get down to business?
Auntie Business?
Barney The money.
Auntie You don't beat about the bush Tom, do you?
Barney I like to get things out of the way.
Auntie That's what I always say. To get things out of the way, kick 'em around and blow 'em away!!!

Barney Bloody hell!

Auntie Now I know you're not a very rich man, Tom.

Barney I wouldn't say that.

Auntie There's nothing wrong in being poor. It's something I approve of. Some of the richest people in the world were poor before they were rich. It's a fact.

Barney Really?

Auntie Oh yes. If you ask me there's too many people with too much money.

Barney I know what you mean.

Auntie I like to, how shall I put it . . .

Barney Any way you like Auntie, any way you like.

Auntie I like to redistribute the wealth.

Barney A sort of Robin Hood?

Auntie Robbing? I'm not robbing anyone. I leave that to the likes of bank robbers. (*She laughs*)

Barney Naturally. But please don't do anything on my account.

Auntie Now don't be proud, Tom. There is nothing wrong with having a lot of money and passing it on to someone less fortunate.

Barney Frankly Auntie, I don't care who gets it.

Auntie After all, if we can't help each other, what is the point to life?

Barney My thoughts exactly.

Auntie Now, are you any good with money?   .

Barney Me? Good Lord no. I bung it all on the horses usually.

Auntie Oh dear. You'd better let my niece handle that side of things then.

Barney I don't want to get involved with your niece, Auntie.

Auntie (*laughing*) A bit late for that isn't it, Tom?

Barney Why?

Auntie She's got her hooks into you now.

Barney She's what!!

Auntie You are going to marry her.

Barney (*jumping up*) WHAT!!! I'm not in the slightest bit interested in her. I keep telling you.

Auntie Well, really!

Barney (*calming down*) I'm sorry, Auntie. I would love to marry your niece but I'm . . . er . . . already spoken for.

Auntie Spoken for?

Barney Yes. To . . . er . . . Muriel.

Auntie Muriel? Who's Muriel?

Barney My fiancée.

Auntie Fiancée!

Barney Yes.

Auntie But what about my niece?

Barney I'm sure she'll meet a nice man. There's plenty of fish in the sea.

Auntie She'll be so disappointed.

Barney I'm sorry. That's the way it is. I was going to give you the money and . . .

Auntie (*standing up and advancing on Tom*) Pay me off!! You've got the

nerve of a lion I must say. Any money you give to me, I shall give straight
to my niece. It will be a tiny compensation for you not marrying her.

Barney Do whatever you want with the money. It's all yours.

Auntie Before I leave I insist on speaking to my niece. Where is she?

Barney (*shrugging shoulders*) She's not here. I thought you'd tied her up in
some kitchen.

Auntie I did no such thing! If you've hurt her in any way . . .

*Suddenly Muriel enters from the kitchen. She carries a tray with two coffee
cups on it*

Muriel I've made the coffee, Barney. (*She sees Auntie*) Oh hello.

Auntie Who are you? And who's Barney?

Barney (*quickly*) This is Muriel. My fiancée. (*He winks at Muriel*)

Muriel Eh? Fiancée?

Barney Yes darling. Don't you remember we got engaged tonight. (*He
winks again*)

Muriel We did?

Barney Yes.

Auntie It's outrageous! And who's Barney?

Muriel (*pointing to Barney*) Barney.

Barney (*to Auntie*) Who mentioned Barney?

Auntie (*pointing to Muriel*) She did. She said "I've made the coffee,
Barney".

Barney Oh yes. "Coffee Barney". It's a blend of coffee beans. We mix our
own.

Auntie Why do you call it "Barney"?

Barney (*quickly*) After our budgie called "Barney".

Both Auntie and Muriel look around the room for a budgie

Auntie Budgie? Where? I see no budgie.

Barney No, he's . . . er . . . not feeling too well. He's poorly. We locked him
in one of the bedrooms.

Auntie Locked him in? What's the matter with him?

Barney It's his beak.

Auntie His beak?

Barney It's broken.

Auntie How terrible.

Barney He can't ring his little bell.

Auntie I've never heard of anything so ridiculous. You should take him to a
vet, not lock him in the bedroom.

Barney We're going to. In the morning. (*He winks at Muriel*) Aren't we
dear?

Muriel Are we?

Barney Of course we are! (*He winks again*)

Muriel I didn't even know you had a budgie.

Barney (*losing patience*) Well now you do!!!

Auntie I insist on seeing the poor bird. (*She starts for the bathroom*)

Barney No! It's not in there. That's the bathroom.

Auntie enters the bathroom regardless. She still carries the large bag she had when she arrived

Muriel Just what is going on here, Barney?
Barney I can't tell you now. Just do as I say. That woman is dangerous.
Muriel That sweet old lady? I don't believe it.
Barney That's just her cover. Don't be fooled. If she thinks Tom's involved an outsider, we'll all end up at the bottom of the river.

Auntie enters from the bathroom, minus her bag

Auntie You sent me in the bathroom.
Muriel You're lucky he didn't put you in the bath.
Auntie Where's the bedroom? I must see the poor creature. (*She starts for the 1st bedroom door*)
Barney (*blocking her way*) Please don't disturb him. He really isn't up to receiving visitors.
Auntie I only wanted to say "hello". I wasn't going to throw a formal reception.
Barney Please. Just leave him alone. It's not only his beak, it's his wings as well. Any sudden excitement might get him in a flap and lead to disastrous consequences.
Auntie (*sitting down on the settee*) Fair enough. But you must get him to a vet.
Barney We will. Don't worry.
Auntie (*changing the subject*) I suppose the flight's cancelled.
Barney I'm afraid so. He sits on his perch all day.
Auntie (*doesn't hear this*) That lovely honeymoon.
Barney (*realizing*) Oh no! We're going to have a honeymoon. (*To Muriel*) Aren't we darling?
Muriel Don't ask me, I'm only the bride.
Auntie You're going to have that honeymoon, (*she points at Muriel*) with her!!!
Barney After the wedding. Yes.
Auntie What about my niece?
Barney (*anything to please*) She can come as well, I suppose.
Auntie (*horrified*) What!!!
Muriel What!
Barney If she's lonely, she can join us. I'm easy.
Auntie I don't believe what I'm hearing.
Muriel Neither do I!
Barney I don't want to seem ungrateful Auntie, but——
Muriel Auntie? Is this your aunt, Barney?
Auntie There she goes again. She called you Barney.
Barney No. She thought you were my "Aunt Barney".
Auntie Your "Aunt Barney"?
Barney Yes. Grandmother wanted a boy.
Auntie I thought Barney was the budgie.
Barney He is. There's a lot of Barneys in my family. We like the name.

Muriel (*can take no more*) If you ask me you're barmy, Barney!

She exits into the kitchen

Auntie Barmy Barney?

Barney My ... er ... brother Barney. He's got a few screws loose. In his head. Muriel gets us confused sometimes. I can't think why.

Auntie If you ask me, you're the one who's crazy. I'm glad my niece is not marrying you. She wouldn't have been happy at all.

Barney All's well that ends well, eh?

Auntie Quite frankly Tom, I am disappointed in you. Apart from calling everyone in your family the ridiculous name of Barney, I find you lacking in moral fibre.

Barney We can't all be perfect, Auntie.

Auntie (*angry*) Don't call me "Auntie" I am not your auntie. (*She stands up and puts on her hat in the fourth wall mirror*)

Barney You asked me to.

Auntie That was when I thought you were marrying my niece. (*She moves to the front door*)

Barney I'm sure she'll meet someone sooner or later.

Auntie (*at the front door*) I trust I shall never see you again, Tom.

Barney I shall be keeping my fingers crossed.

Auntie (*waving finger at Barney*) You are a blackguard, sir.

Auntie exits

A nerve-strained Barney collapses into a chair

Muriel enters from the kitchen, putting on her coat as she moves to the front door

Barney Muriel! What are you doing?

Muriel I'm going home. I've had enough.

Barney You can't do that. We haven't done anything yet. I mean, what about our dinner?

Muriel (*turning at the front door*) I don't know how you get your kicks Barney, but you're not going to get them from me.

Barney (*standing up*) You don't understand.

Muriel I understand enough to realize you're some kind of lunatic.

Barney I am not a lunatic!

Muriel No normal man would say that I was his fiancée. (*She thinks about what she has just said*)

Barney Look, I had to say that. The stupid woman wanted me to marry her niece!

Muriel I can't think why.

Barney They're dangerous people these gangsters. You don't mess about with them.

Muriel (*shocked*) Gangsters!

Barney That's right. She came for the money.

Muriel (*totally lost*) What money?

Barney This money! (*He opens the drinks cabinet. He pulls out bundles of cash*) Oh my God! She's forgotten it!

Muriel Where did you get all that?

Barney It's not mine.

Muriel Whose is it?

Barney Who cares? Auntie wanted it, and now she's left it behind.

Muriel (*moving to the drinks cabinet and picking up a bundle of notes*) There's an awful lot of money here.

Barney They'll send somebody back for it. It will probably be "Uncle" this time.

Muriel Uncle who?

Barney How the hell should I know?

Muriel (*taking her coat off*) Now Barney dear, let's get this straight ...

Barney I thought you were leaving.

Muriel I just want to sort this money out. After all we mustn't rush things, must we?

The doorbell rings

Barney (*in total panic*) Oh my God! It's Uncle! In two minutes I'll be deaf.

Muriel Don't you mean dead?

Barney That as well.

Muriel (*holding up money*) What shall I do with this money?

Barney Quickly. Put it back in the cabinet.

They stuff the money back into the drinks cabinet. The doorbell rings again

Muriel Where shall I go?

Barney If you value your hearing go and hide in the bathroom.

Muriel (*moving to the bathroom door*) With Barney the Budgie?

Barney No, he's in the bedroom. No he's not. There is no budgie. Now move!!

Muriel exits into the bathroom

Barney takes a deep breath and moves to the front door. He opens it and throws himself backwards against the wall with his eyes shut and his hands over his ears

Auntie comes charging in

(*Opening his eyes*) You again!

Auntie I've come for my money.

Barney I'll get it for you. (*He moves to the drinks cabinet*)

Auntie It was intended as a honeymoon gift for you and my niece.

Barney (*opening the drinks cabinet*) Don't start all that again. You can have all of it. Every penny.

Auntie I should jolly well think so.

Barney (*passing bundles of notes to Auntie*) Here you are. And good riddance.

Auntie What's all this? (*She puts the bundles down on the desk top*)

Barney The money you came for. It's all yours.

Auntie This isn't my money. (*She pushes the money across the desk to Barney*)

Barney I don't care whose money it is, or where it came from. Take it. It's causing too many problems. (*He pushes the money back to Auntie*)

Auntie I don't want it. (*She pushes the money back to Barney*) I want the other money.

Barney I haven't got any more money. I'm not the Bank of flaming England!

Auntie Are you trying to pay me off!

Barney Just take the money and run woman! (*He pushes the money back to Auntie*)

Suddenly Muriel enters from the bathroom. She is carrying Auntie's bag

Muriel I found this in the bathroom. (*She pulls banknotes out of the bag*) It's absolutely full of money!

Auntie (*pointing at the bag*) *That* is my money.

Barney *Your* money?

Auntie Twenty thousand dollars. I was going to give it to you and my niece to spend on your honeymoon.

Barney For once and for all, I am not in the slightest bit interested in your niece.

Auntie So you keep telling me. That is why you're not getting any money. (*To Muriel*) That money belongs to me. Please give it back this instant.

Barney Let me see that. (*He grabs the bag. It breaks open and dozens of banknotes fall on to the top of the desk*) Oh my God!

Auntie I can't stand it any more. (*She shouts*) Give me my money! GIVE ME MY MONEY!!! (*She thuds her fist down on the desk but accidentally hits the desk top fan switch. All the notes go flying into the air like a snowstorm*)

Muriel Good heavens!

Auntie Good gracious!

Barney Good God!

The three of them run around all over the stage grabbing at the notes

Muriel We don't know whose money is whose.

Barney We can divide it up later. (*He turns the fan off*)

Auntie It belongs to me. The money and the plates are mine.

Barney⎫
Muriel⎭ (*together*) What plates?

Auntie Some beautiful Spode plates. In my bag.

Muriel (*aside*) Are you sure she's a gangster, Barney?

Barney She's probably just knocked over an antique shop.

They are picking up as many notes as possible. Auntie is shoving them into her bag. Barney is putting them into the drinks cabinet and Muriel is stuffing them inside the top of her dress. Barney suddenly notices this

What the hell are you doing, Muriel?

Muriel I'm getting my share.

Barney What are you on about? It's not your money.

Muriel You don't know whose money it is.

Auntie It's *my* money!

Muriel (*still putting money inside the front of her dress*) It's the chance of a lifetime! All this money and no-one knows who it belongs to. I'm off.

Barney Where are you going?

Muriel (*gathering coat and moving to front door*) To spend it.

Barney You can't!

Muriel I bet I can. See you around Barney. (*She opens the front door to exit*)

Tom and Alice are standing outside about to enter. They are carrying their suitcases

Gordon bleedin' Bennett!

Tom What the hell is going on?

Alice Auntie! What are you doing? I'd forgotten all about you.

Auntie Alice! Thank goodness you're here. (*She points at Tom*) Who's he?

Alice My fiancé. You haven't met him yet, have you?

Auntie You're engaged again so soon. (*To Barney*) You won't have to marry her now, Tom.

Tom (*puzzled*) Why not?

Auntie (*pointing to Barney*) I was talking to him. (*She turns to Tom*) Who are you?

Tom I'm his brother.

Auntie (*horrified*) Barmy Barney!! Oh God!! (*To Alice*) You're getting married to Barmy Barney! His screws are loose!! (*She faints into the arms of Alice*)

The CURTAIN falls quickly

Elvis Presley songs should be played throughout the interval over the theatre PA

ACT II

The same. The action is continuous
Alice is bending over Auntie trying to revive her. The other three look on

Tom What the hell is going on here, Barney?
Barney I thought you were on your way to Miami.
Tom The fog hasn't lifted yet. Now what has been——
Alice Tom! Help me get Auntie into the bedroom.
Barney (*to Alice*) You know Auntie?
Alice Of course I do.
Tom She phoned to say she was coming around to sort out the money.
Alice I completely forgot. This is all my fault.
Tom (*to Barney*) Did she bring any money?
Barney No . . . yes.
Alice Will you two stop nattering. Come and help me, Tom. Grab Auntie's
legs.

*Tom picks up Auntie's legs and Alice carries her by the shoulders. They lift her
to the 2nd bedroom door*

(*To Tom*) You'd better bring some brandy to revive her.

*Tom leans over to pick up the brandy bottle from the drinks cabinet, but as it
would mean dropping Auntie's legs, he can't quite manage it*

Barney Let me do that, Tom.

*Barney picks up the brandy bottle from the drinks cabinet and takes a large
swig before tucking it under Tom's arm*

Tom Barney! That was an expensive bottle of brandy.
Barney (*winking heavily*) We're not exactly penniless, are we?
Alice Come on, Tom.
Tom (*to Barney*) I'll sort you out in a minute. (*He points at Muriel*) And
who's she?
Barney Muriel.
Tom Muriel?
Barney Directory Enquiries. We were going to make a connection.

Muriel gives Barney a rude glare

Tom I've got a few enquiries of my own. Don't either of you go away.
Barney Oh we weren't going anywhere, were we Muriel?

Muriel gives him another nasty look and sits down in a chair

Alice (*opening the 2nd bedroom door*) This way, Tom.

Alice and Tom, carrying Auntie, exit into the 2nd bedroom

Barney That way, Tom. (*He slams the door behind him*) Come on Muriel, given me that money.
Muriel Not bloody likely.
Barney It doesn't belong to you. (*He advances on Muriel*)
Muriel No and it doesn't belong to you.
Barney Hand it over!
Muriel No!
Barney I'll count to three Muriel. One, two, three . . .

The 2nd bedroom door opens and Tom enters

Tom (*to Barney*) Did she bring any money?
Barney There's money everywhere you look.
Tom What do you mean?
Barney There's her money, there's the other stuff . . .
Tom What other stuff?
Barney The bank-job money.
Tom What bank job?
Barney (*winking heavily*) You know, the "if I could do anything in life, I would rob a bank", bank job.

Muriel leans over intently to try and catch the conversation

Tom (*thinking Barney has robbed the bank*) Good God! You haven't! I don't believe it!

Alice appears at the door of the 2nd bedroom

Alice Tom. Can you come in here. I think Auntie may be coming round. It would be nice if she could see someone familiar when she wakes up. (*She gives Muriel a nasty look*)
Tom I'm not sure about that. She's only met me once before and she fainted.
Alice Well hold your hands over your face or something!
Tom Charming.

Tom and Alice exit into the 2nd bedroom

Barney Now come on, Muriel. (*He holds out his hand*) Money.
Muriel No.

The telephone rings. Barney answers it. During the conversation he stands behind Muriel and tries to retrieve the money from inside the top of her dress. On each attempt she slaps his hand and he fails

Barney (*on the phone*) Hello. . . . Who? . . . What airline? . . . I see. . . . This is Mr Weals. . . . I'm his brother. . . . Yes. . . . He must check in within the next hour. . . . Yes. . . . Leave it to me. . . . I'll see he gets the message. . . . Not at all. . . . Goodbye. (*He replaces the receiver*)
Muriel Who was that?
Barney The airport. They say the fog's lifted. Tom's flight to Miami is on.

Muriel What about all this money then? Perhaps it belongs to him.
Barney It must do. (*He shakes his head*) It's just not like him.
Muriel What isn't?
Barney (*spilling the beans*) It's just not like Tom to rob a bank.
Muriel Rob a bank!
Barney Yes.
Muriel Your brother has robbed a bank! (*She starts emptying all the money out of the top of her dress*) This money I'm stealing isn't legal! I could go to prison for stealing stolen money! Why didn't you tell me?
Barney Where did you think all this money came from?
Muriel I thought he'd been saving up! With his piggy bank.
Barney I blame myself, Muriel. It's all my fault.
Muriel What did you do? Drive the getaway car?
Barney No, no I said his life lacked adventure. He said it didn't. He claimed he'd done something daring. This is it. He's robbed a bank and it's all my fault.
Muriel How?
Barney I put the idea in his head. Doing a bank was always something I wanted to do.
Muriel Next time recommend a walking holiday in the Himalayas.
Barney And now he's got all this money to deal with.
Muriel (*picking up a few notes*) We could help him with that.
Barney I think he's getting all the help he needs from these gangsters, Muriel.
Muriel This "Auntie" person you mean?
Barney Even Alice knew her, that's what I don't understand. How long has this been going on?
Muriel Don't ask me.
Barney It has to be organized crime. Auntie must be the Godfather.
Muriel (*puzzled*) The Godfather?
Barney Tom's asking for trouble. I've got to help him. He is my brother. (*He starts for the 2nd bedroom door*)
Muriel Brotherly love?
Barney That's right, brotherly love.
Muriel (*picking up a bundle of money*) There's such a lot of money here.
Barney (*stopping at the door*) Yes. You can say that again.
Muriel I always say that families should share things.
Barney What do you mean?
Muriel All this money. You should keep half of it.
Barney I couldn't. It belongs to Tom. He went out and earned it.
Muriel Nicked it more like. It was your idea after all.
Barney You've got a point there.
Muriel If you hadn't suggested it, he would never have done it.
Barney (*opening the drinks cabinet*) Well, maybe if I just took a little for services rendered. I do deserve something.
Muriel Of course you do. He'll never miss it. (*She takes out some of the bundles from the drinks cabinet*)
Barney Exactly. We'll have to be quick though.

They take all the cash from inside the drinks cabinet and put it down on the coffee table

(*Counting the bundles out*) One for Tom, two for me. One for Tom, three for me. One for Tom ...

Muriel Don't bother counting, just estimate. (*She stuffs money into Barney's pockets*)

Barney You've changed your tune, haven't you?

Muriel I'll help you steal the money on one condition.

Barney And what's that?

Muriel You spend it all on me.

Barney It's a deal. Now what shall we put the money in?

Muriel (*looking around the room*) What about those two suitcases?

Barney Good idea. We'll throw out their contents and then get out of here.

They each unlock a case and turn them upside down over the settee. The original money comes cascading out

Oh my God! More money! He's robbed another bank, Muriel.

Muriel Gordon Bennett!

Barney They didn't go to the airport at all. The Bonnie and Clyde of suburbia!!

Muriel Gordon Bennett!

Barney What shall we do?

They face each other absolutely speechless

Muriel ⎫
Barney ⎬ (*together*) Take the bloody lot!!!

They now stuff the remainder of the money into the cases and shut them

Muriel A thought has just occurred to me, Barney. (*She picks up Alice's handbag and opens it*)

Barney What?

Muriel (*taking out the airline tickets*) Why don't we make sure we're not caught.

Barney Use his airline tickets? We can't!

Muriel We'll get on that flight to Miami. He won't know that the airport rang. We'll be out of the country before he realizes what's going on.

Barney That is very dishonest, Muriel.

Muriel So is stealing all this money.

Barney Tom won't like it at all. He was going on his honeymoon.

Muriel Honeymoon? You said it was just a holiday.

Barney Just a little lie, Muriel. This isn't my flat either, it's his. Oh what does it matter anyway? We'll use his tickets. He can always buy some more. Leave him some money behind.

Muriel (*opening the case*) I'll leave a few thousand dollars. He can go First Class. (*She stuffs a bundle of money into Alice's handbag*)

Barney Is your passport up to date?

Muriel Yes.

Barney Good. So is mine. We'll stop off and pick them up on the way. Right, let's go, before they come back.

Muriel What about my shift at eight?

Barney Send them a postcard.

Muriel (*starting for the front door, picking up her coat on the way*) Right. How exciting! I'm a criminal.

Barney And a very pretty one.

They kiss each other and carrying their two cases exit through the front door

Tom and Alice enter from the 2nd bedroom

Tom Barney, I want a word with you ... (*He sees the empty room*) Oh, he's gone.

Alice Good.

Tom I wonder where he's gone?

Alice I don't know and I don't care. I can't imagine what he said to Auntie. She's out stone cold.

Tom She'll be all right. It's Barney I'm worried about.

Alice I wouldn't worry about him. (*She sits down on the settee*) How did he get in anyway?

Tom I gave him a key. In case of emergencies. (*He takes his quiff off*)

Alice It's only an emergency if he gets in. Not before.

Tom If only that Mr Pintocelli had been at the hotel. We could have given him his money and got back here before Auntie arrived.

Alice I still think you should have left the money with the hotel reception.

Tom Hand over half a million dollars to the night porter? Not likely.

Alice Not everyone's as dishonest as you'd like to think, Tom.

Tom Well you are for a start. Look how firm I had to be with you to make sure we returned *all* the money.

Alice Er ... yes.

Tom You wanted to keep some of it. I had to put my foot down. You have to fight temptation in an event like this.

Alice Of course dear.

Tom We'll have to swop suitcases at the airport tomorrow.

Alice Yes. I suppose so.

Tom I'm surprised he hasn't been around here. He must have seen our address on the cases. And surely he would notice that he was half a million dollars short. Anyone would notice that.

Alice You'd think so.

Tom Anyway, tomorrow he'll have it all back. He can count the notes in the departure lounge.

Alice (*worried*) Do you think he'll count every note dear?

Tom I would if I was him. (*He moves to the drinks cabinet*) Drink, darling?

Alice Yes. (*She remembers she hid money in the cabinet*) No!!!

Tom What's it to be dear? Yes or no?

Alice Why don't we ... er ... have a cup of tea instead?

Tom No thanks. I want a drink. A real drink.

Alice Well I don't. I want a cup of tea. One of your special blends.

Tom Have a cup of tea, Alice. I'm going to pour myself a stiff Cinzano. (*He begins to open the drinks cabinet door*)

Alice (*jumping up*) DON'T TOUCH THOSE DRINKS!!!

Tom (*stopping*) Why ever not?

Alice (*moving to Tom*) Because . . . because a cup of tea would be so much better for you.

Tom I don't think so, Alice. You know what happens when I have a cup of tea

Alice No. What happens?

Tom (*squirming*) You know . . . I have to . . . and go to the . . . you know, Alice. It always affects me that way.

Alice I didn't know that. (*She laughs*)

Tom It's the same with cod fillets!

Alice Cod fillets? We'll make the tea very weak then.

Tom If it's all the same with you, I'd rather have a drink and sit down in that chair. I don't want to upset my rhythm. I'll only risk a cup of tea on very special occasions. (*He slides open the drinks cabinet door*)

Alice (*shouting*) TODAY IS MY BIRTHDAY!!! (*She slams the cabinet door shut and traps Tom's hand*)

Tom (*in pain*) Aaaah! That hurt! Why did you do that? I think you've broken my hand! (*He moves around the room holding his injured hand*) I won't be able to use the cheese slicer at work.

Alice I'm so sorry, darling. I didn't mean to hurt you.

Tom I'm going to go and put it under cold water.

Tom exits into the kitchen

Alice That's a good idea, Tom. (*She slides back the cabinet door*)

Tom pokes his head through the serving hatch

Alice slams the cabinet door shut again

Tom And another thing. Your birthday isn't until the fifteenth of next month.

Alice Oh how silly of me. I could have sworn it was the fifteenth of this month.

Tom No. The fifteenth of this month was meant to be our wedding day.

Tom disappears, closing the serving hatch

Alice immediately slides open the drinks cabinet door and sees that her money has gone

Alice Oh my God! The money's gone! (*She slides the door open and closes it two or three times. She can't believe the money has gone*) Somebody's taken my money!

Tom comes running out of the kitchen. He has a wet towel wrapped around his hand

Tom What's going on? What's all the noise?

Alice (*in panic*) The money's been stolen!

Tom Nonsense. It's in the cases over there. (*He turns to where the cases should be*) Oh my God! They've gone! Half a million dollars belonging to Mr Chillypunto!

Alice Pintocelli!

Tom (*in panic*) Pintochewy! Puntochoppy!

Alice His name is Pintocelli.

Tom I don't care what his name is. I've lost his money. Who could have taken that money?

Alice }
Tom } (*together*) Barney!!!

Tom He stole our cases.

Alice And that girl.

Tom Muriel?

Alice I knew she was that type. I could see it in her eyes.

Tom What type?

Alice The sort who wants to run off with all the money.

Tom Oh, you mean your sort?

Alice We've been robbed Tom, robbed. All our money gone.

Tom Be fair dear. It wasn't all our money. In fact none of it was our money. Most of it belongs to Mr Pintowhateverhisnameis.

Alice It's all gone! The bloody lot!

Tom And the rest of it was from the bank robbery.

Alice What bank robbery?

Tom Oh ... er ... Barney robbed a bank.

Alice WHAT!!!

Tom Afraid so. It's all my fault. I put the idea in his head.

Alice You did what!

Tom It was when we were kids. We were discussing what we wanted to do when we were grown up. I said I wanted a cooking badge. Barney had to go one better. He said he wanted to rob a bank. I'll never forgive myself.

Alice (*none the wiser*) What are you talking about, Tom?

Tom He thinks I'm unadventurous.

Alice You are.

Tom Barney was scared of living a dull life.

Alice Compared to you, he's like James Bond!

Tom (*very emotional*) It's all my fault. Oh Barney, Barney, Barney. What have I done to you? (*He flops down on to a chair*)

The 2nd bedroom door opens and Auntie enters. She is swaying and carrying the empty bottle of brandy in her hand

Auntie Barney? Has anyone seen Barney? (*She looks around the room for the budgie*)

Alice (*going over to Auntie*) Auntie! Are you all right?

Auntie He's not in the bedroom. He must have got out.

Tom He's gone, Auntie.

Auntie Gone?

Tom With all the money.

Auntie (*incredulous*) Barney has? What money?

Alice (*slowly and deliberately*) The bird has flown, Auntie.

Auntie I thought he was having trouble doing that.

Tom What is she on about? (*He sees the empty brandy bottle*) Oh no! The brandy!

Alice (*seeing it too*) I don't believe it.

Tom She's drunk the lot!

Alice It was meant to revive her.

Tom Revive her? That lot could revive the dead!

Auntie Dead? Who's dead? Is Barney dead? The poor little thing.

Alice No. No-one's dead, Auntie. Tom was just saying that you shouldn't have drunk all his brandy. Not all in one go. It's not good for you.

Auntie (*waving the bottle in the air*) I don't care what Tom thinks. He's a total degenerate!

Alice Auntie!

Tom Well, really! (*He stands up*)

Auntie (*to Alice*) He doesn't want to marry you, you know.

Alice What!

Tom I do want to marry her.

Auntie I know *you* want to, but Tom wants to marry Muriel.

Alice Muriel? (*To Tom*) Is this true?

Tom Of course it isn't. I don't want to marry Muriel. I don't even know her.

Auntie (*to Alice*) Tom wants to take you on his honeymoon.

Alice I know that, Auntie. It'll be tomorrow if the fog lifts.

Auntie But he wants to take you *and* Muriel! He wants three in a bed! The swine!

Alice (*horrified*) Tom! Is this true?

Tom I don't know what she's babbling on about. She's mad. Raving bloody looney!

Auntie (*to Alice*) You must be careful dear. He wants to tie you up in the kitchen——

Tom What!!

Auntie —whilst he makes his "Coffee Barney".

Alice ⎱ (*together*) "Coffee Barney"?
Tom ⎰

Auntie It's his own blend. He likes to mix his beans.

Tom What?

Alice Auntie, what are you talking about?

Auntie And then there's his brother "Barmy Barney". (*She points at Tom*) I've heard about him.

Alice What about him?

Tom Yes. What about him ... er ... me?

Auntie He's got a few screws loose.

Alice (*looking at Tom*) What!

Tom I have not!

Alice (*to Auntie*) Who told you that?

Auntie Tom did.

Tom I did not!

Auntie (*to Tom*) I know *you* didn't. I'm talking about that scoundrel Tom.

Alice (*pointing at Tom*) Auntie, this *is* Tom.
Auntie No dear, this is Barmy Barney. He's got loose screws in his head.
  (*She puts her fingers to her head to suggest he's mad*)
Tom I have not!
Alice Auntie, you're getting very confused.
Tom I'm not surprised. She's finished the bottle.
Alice What are we going to do?
Tom I'm going to look for Barney. (*He moves to the front door*)
Auntie He won't have got very far.
Tom (*stopping at the door*) And how would you know?
Auntie He's hurt himself.
Alice Barney has?
Auntie He can't ring the bell any more.
Tom Of course he can. I got it fixed last week. It's working perfectly.
Auntie It's all very well for you Barmy Barney, but try ringing it with your
  beak! (*She taps him on his nose*)
Tom (*totally confused*) With my what?
Alice (*taking Auntie's arm*) I think you'd better go and lie down, Auntie.
  Sleep it off.
Tom Good idea. Don't come out for a week.
Auntie (*breaking away from Alice*) I don't want to go to bed. I want to go to
  a party and whoop it up!!!
Alice } (*together*) { I think you should go to bed dear.
Tom } { A party? That's not a very good idea.
Auntie I don't want to go to bed! I want to play games. (*Her eyes slowly turn
  towards Tom*) Mad, crazy sex games. Let's go for it! Let's go for it!

*Auntie chases Tom round the room. Alice tries to hold her back. Tom dives on
to the settee, followed by Auntie, followed by Alice*

*Tom rolls on to the floor in front of the settee and then runs into the 2nd
bedroom slamming the door behind him*

Tom (*off*) Keep her away from me, Alice. She's bonkers!
Alice Keep still, Auntie. (*She grabs hold of Auntie*)
Auntie (*wriggling like mad*) I want to play. Let me go.

The doorbell rings. They freeze

Alice Who can that be?

*Tom enters from the 2nd bedroom. He keeps a beady eye on Auntie and
stays close to the wall*

Tom Maybe it's Barney, with all the money.

Auntie gets to her feet

Auntie Get the cage ready. We must lock him up.
Alice (*to Auntie*) Lock who up?
Auntie Barney of course. Who else?

Tom If it is him, I won't lock him up, I'll knock him out. (*He starts for the door*) I'll crush him with my own hands!

Alice (*following him*) Be careful, Tom.

Auntie Barmy! Come here! (*She runs over to Tom and starts pounding on his chest*) You're a great big oversize bully. Leave poor little Barney alone.

The doorbell rings again

> *Tom lifts up Auntie off her feet and carries her off into the 2nd bedroom. Alice follows them in*

> *Tom re-enters on his own and slams the door shut behind him*

Tom I'm coming. I'm coming. (*In the confusion he looks in the fourth-wall mirror and puts his quiff on back-to-front. He tries to correct it as he opens the front door*)

> *Frankie, one of Mr Pintocelli's gangsters, stands there. He is about six foot six and built like a tank. He has a disturbing habit of cracking his knuckles. He's not very clever either*

(*Slightly nervous*) Hello. Can I ... er help you?

Frankie grunts and walks straight in, completely ignoring Tom. He looks around the room and walks over to the window. Tom shuts the door and follows him

Are you ... are you someone I know?

Frankie That depends, dun it?

Tom Depends? Depends on what?

Frankie Whether you watch the telly.

Tom Occasionally. Have you been on it? (*He is still moving his quiff*)

Frankie I'm always on it.

Tom How very nice for you. Look, you just can't come barging in here. This is my flat.

Frankie I do what I like mate. (*He cracks his knuckles*) Now, guess where you've seen me on the telly.

Tom I don't know. (*He still plays with his quiff*)

Frankie Go on, have a guess.

Tom No. (*He gives up on the quiff. It now sticks out at an angle*)

Frankie I'll be fair. I'll give you, (*he counts out on 4 fingers*), three guesses.

Tom (*losing patience*) I don't want to guess.

Frankie You'd better. Or I'll smash your kneecaps!

Tom immediately covers his knees with his hands in criss-cross fashion

Tom OK, OK. (*He thinks hard*) One of those wildlife programmes. With the gorillas?

Frankie No. (*He cracks his knuckles*)

Tom No, no, of course not. Silly me. How about one of those kid's shows where they ape around?

Frankie No. (*He cracks his knuckles*) One more guess, mate.

Tom Oh dear. Last guess. (*He thinks hard*) The late night horror film?

Frankie shakes his head

In that case I give up.

Frankie You give up?

Tom Yes. Absolutely.

Frankie (*proudly*) Police Five.

Tom Police Five?

Frankie (*happy to find a fan*) I was on it last week.

Tom (*worried*) Were you really? (*He sits down on the settee*)

Frankie (*fixing Tom with a steely glare*) Twelve thousand pinball machines fell off the back of a lorry in the Old Kent Road.

Tom Good Lord! Imagine the mess!

Frankie Anyway, business first. (*He sits in the chair*)

Tom Business?

Frankie (*cracking his knuckles*) I've come for the money.

Tom Money?

Frankie This is flat number eleven, isn't it?

Tom Yes.

Frankie I want the money then.

Tom What money?

Frankie Stop messin' about, mate. Hand over the readies and I'll be on me bike.

Tom What? Where have you left it? In the downstairs hall?

Frankie Left what?

Tom Your bike. I don't want a filthy bike cluttering up my hallway.

Frankie I ain't got a real bike, stupid. It's an expression.

Tom An expression?

Frankie Yeah. Like "I'm going to break your bloody neck". (*He cracks his knuckles*)

Tom Oh that type of expression.

Frankie So where's me money?

Tom I haven't got it. You must have the wrong address.

Frankie He rang you up.

Tom Who did?

Frankie The Guvner. He told you we was coming over.

Tom We?

Frankie Me and the boys. We'd 'ave been here earlier but we got lost in the fog.

Tom I see. Well I'm sorry to disappoint you but he didn't speak to me. It must have been somebody else.

Frankie (*menacingly*) Are you messing me about?

Tom No.

Frankie No-one messes Frankie about.

Tom Is that so? I haven't actually met this Frankie, so I couldn't say.

Frankie *I* am Frankie!

Tom (*grinning falsely*) Oh you're Frankie.

Frankie (*rising and moving over to Tom*) And you seem to think you're some kind of comedian. (*He grabs Tom's collar and lifts him off the ground*) A bit of a laugh are you?

Tom (*terrified*) Laugh? I don't know who you are. I'm not laughing. Laugh? I should be in Miami. On my honeymoon and attending the Convention.

Frankie (*this stops him*) The Convention? (*He thinks of gangsters*)

Tom Yes.

Frankie (*smiling*) That's different. (*He lets go of Tom*) I didn't know you were going to the Convention.

Tom I was looking forward to it. We were going to discuss all kinds of things.

Frankie Like what?

Tom Well, see a few films, ask a few questions.

Frankie Discuss the hits?

Tom Naturally.

Frankie Check up on each other's records?

Tom Find out who's got what, of course.

Frankie (*sadly*) I wanted to go myself, but the Guvner wants me to stay here and keep an eye on things.

Tom What a pity. The highlight this year is meeting the "Memphis Mob".

Frankie (*in ecstasy*) Ah! The "Memphis Mob".

Tom It was going to be a wonderful week. We were going to hear all the facts. See film clips of the old days. Everything.

Frankie (*now getting nostalgic*) The good old days. Lovely.

Tom They were the best.

Frankie Too right. The best bit of course, is getting to wear a tuxedo.

Tom I prefer blue suede shoes myself.

Frankie Was the ... was the *MAN* himself going to be there?

Tom (*looking at him suspiciously*) Well hardly.

Frankie (*tapping his nose*) I heard a rumour he was going to show this year.

Tom (*excited*) Oh you mean the seance! Well we can always try I suppose.

Frankie (*alarmed*) Seance?

Tom You know. You all join hands and the table floats up into the air. Then someone says, (*in very deep voice*), "Is there anybody there?".

Frankie (*shocked*) That's for dead people.

Tom Of course it is. We wouldn't be asking if there was anybody there if they were alive and we could see them. Would we?

Frankie You mean ... you mean that the *MAN* is dead?

Tom (*looking at Frankie like he is crazy*) Of course he's dead. Ate too many hamburgers. Keeled over.

Frankie (*can't take this in*) What?

Tom You must have heard about it.

Frankie Not a whisper. (*He rubs his eyes*) You'll have to excuse me. I can't believe it.

Tom I understand. It affected me that way too.

Frankie Have you got a phone?

Tom (*pointing to the telephone*) Over there.

Frankie I must tell the Guvner that the *MAN* is dead.

Tom I expect he already knows.

Frankie (*dialling the number*) I still can't believe it. (*To Tom*) Would you mind? This is a private call.

Tom Of course. I'll go and make some coffee. Then maybe we could discuss the hits. I'll bring you up to date on everything.

Frankie Perhaps. Make mine a cup of tea.

Tom (*starting for the kitchen*) Tea for two then. Actually, I won't have any. It makes ... well. It doesn't agree with me. Upsets my rhythm. (*He squirms*) I've always been troubled ...

Frankie Get out!!!

Tom Right.

He scurries off into the kitchen

Frankie (*on the phone*) Mr Pintocelli's suite please. (*He catches his reflection in the fourth-wall mirror, snarls in a threatening manner*). ... Is that you Guvner? ... It's me Frankie boy—I'm around that guy Weals' place. ... I haven't got the money yet but I'm working on it. ... He was on his way to the Convention too—just like you Guv. ... The thing is, have you heard the news? ... The *MAN*, Guv. ... He's snuffed it. ... No, it wasn't a hit—he ate too many hamburgers and keeled over. ... I know Guv, very sad. ... We'll have to show some respect. ... Perhaps a week's free protection for everyone. ... Don't worry Guv, I'll get the money off him. ... He's playing hard to get, but I can play harder. I've got the place surrounded by the boys. ... He won't get away, Guv. ... Leave it to Frankie. ... That's me, Guv. ... I'm Frankie—right. See you. (*He replaces the phone*) Pillock! (*To himself*) I better check on the boys. They might be getting bored.

He exits through the front door

Tom, singing a line from "Hound Dog", enters from the kitchen with two cups on a tray

Alice enters from the 2nd bedroom

Alice I don't want the tea now, Tom.

Tom It's not for you. It's for Frankie. (*He looks in the bathroom for Frankie*)

Alice Who's Frankie?

Tom He's a big bloke.

Alice What does he do?

Tom He's an Elvis Presley fan like me. (*He looks in the 2nd bedroom*)

Auntie (*off*) Have you found Barney?

Tom No I haven't!! (*He slams the door shut*)

Alice (*sarcastically*) How wonderful. But why did he come here?

Tom We were going to discuss the hits. Where's he gone? (*He looks in the 1st bedroom*)

Alice (*impatiently*) What did he want, Tom?

Tom sits down on the settee and puts the tray on the coffee table

Tom He wanted the money.

Alice The bank robbery money? Is he a policeman?

Tom How should I know?

Alice How did he know we have any money?

Tom We don't have any money.

Alice How did he know we had any then?

Tom Don't ask me. (*He stands up*)

Alice They must be surrounding the place.

Tom looks out of the window

Can you see anyone?

Tom It's still a little foggy, but yes, there's someone ... and another. They're wearing plain clothes.

Alice Oh dear!

Tom They're standing in Mrs Smith's garden.

Alice Are they incognito?

Tom No, they're in Mrs Smith's garden!

Alice No. I meant are they immersed and hidden in the crowd?

Tom There is no crowd. Just five coppers standing in Mrs Smith's front garden. For a policeman he was very knowledgeable about the Convention.

Alice What did he say to you?

Tom That the best thing was getting to wear a tuxedo.

Alice Not the Convention! About the money.

Tom He said someone rang up and told me he was coming over.

Alice Who rang up?

Tom I think he said it was his governor.

Alice That means his Chief Inspector. Did you take the call?

Tom Of course not.

Alice Then it must have been when we were out. It must have been ...

Alice }
Tom } (*together*)   Barney!!!

Alice I always said that brother of yours was no good. He's landed you in it this time.

Tom What do you mean?

Alice Barney must have told the police that you stole the money.

Tom Why on earth would he do that?

Alice To take the heat off him, so he could make a getaway.

Tom So this bloke Frankie is a policeman.

Alice More than likely. Did he say *anything* that would indicate he was?

Tom I don't know.

Alice Think Tom. Think!

Tom He did mention the "Boys".

Alice That would be his Division. The boys in blue. Anything else?

Tom He mentioned his "Police Five".

Alice Probably five trained marksmen surrounding the building. We know where they are. (*She points at the window*) In Mrs Smith's garden.

Tom Hell's bells!

Alice More like Sweeney Todd.

Tom Sweeney Todd?

Alice Flying Squad!

Tom Oh my God!

Alice But where's he gone now?

Tom He used the phone. Said it was to his governor.

Alice He's gone to the top for more reinforcements.

Tom Oh no!! We're heading for "Jailhouse Rock"!

Alice Tom, we are in trouble. The police are on to us. They want the money. We haven't got the money. Barney has, and God alone knows where he is. The shifty-eyed snake.

Tom What shall we do, Alice?

Alice Let's make a run for it.

Tom And get shot down by marksmen?

Alice We'll use the side entrance. The one that leads into the alleyway.

Tom They'll be watching that.

Alice It's a chance we'll have to take. Get the airline tickets. We'll sleep at the airport and catch the first flight to Miami in the morning.

Tom This is ridiculous, Alice. We haven't done anything!

Alice You know that, I know that. But the police think we have. And then there's Mr Pintocelli, we've lost his five hundred thousand dollars.

Tom I see your point.

Alice Now get those tickets.

Tom But what happens if we bump into him at the airport?

Alice We'll hide in the toilet on the plane.

Tom All the way to Miami, stuck in a toilet!

Alice Bring something to read. Now get the tickets out of my bag.

Tom (*searching Alice's handbag*) Alice, Alice. They've gone. (*He looks again*) Somebody's stolen our air tickets!!

Alice |
Tom | (*together*) Barney!

Tom I'll never forgive him. Not only has he run off with all the money, but he's gone on my honeymoon as well!!

Alice Never mind him now. He's left some money behind. (*She takes a bundle of notes out of her handbag*) We'll buy new tickets at the airport.

Tom Right.

Alice grabs her coat and they move to the front door

What about Auntie?

Alice Oh my God! I'd forgotten her.

Tom You can't just leave her.

Alice We'll have to take her with us.

Tom What! All the way to Miami? Three in a toilet?

Alice We'll bung her on a shuttle flight to Glasgow. She always wanted to visit Scotland.

Tom Go and get her then. (*He moves to the window*) I'll look out the window for the Sweeney Plods.

Alice Sweeney Todd! Flying Squad!

Alice exits into the 2nd bedroom

Tom (*looking cautiously out of window*) I hope they hold the Elvis Convention in London next year.

Alice enters from the 2nd bedroom dragging Auntie by her shoulders

Alice Come on, Tom. I can't carry her alone.
Tom (*moving over to Auntie*) I'll get her feet.

He picks up her feet. They start carrying her to the front door

This is all Barney's fault.
Auntie (*waking up*) Barney? Have you found Barney?
Tom Oh God! She's off!
Alice No Auntie. Barney's on his way to Miami.
Auntie He'll never get there. It's too far! The poor little mite will get so exhausted.
Tom He's got our tickets!
Auntie They'll eat anything you know! If they're unhappy.
Alice As soon as the fog lifts, up he'll go.
Auntie You shouldn't have kept him cooped up for so long. It's your own fault.
Alice What?
Tom She's talking double dutch again.
Alice Auntie. We're going to the airport.
Auntie Bottle of port? Good idea. (*She leans over and picks up a bottle of port from the drinks cabinet. She takes a swig from it before anyone can stop her. She then passes out*)
Tom I'm not sure this is such a good idea, Alice.
Alice I can't leave her here. Now open the front door.

Tom opens the front door and then, holding Auntie's legs, walks through it backwards. He bumps straight into ...

Frankie who is about to enter

Frankie Hello, hello, hello. What's going on here then?
Tom We were just ... er ...
Alice Just taking Auntie for a walk, weren't we, darling?
Tom Yes. That's right officer, er Frankie. Just giving Auntie a constitutional.
Frankie Looks like she should be institutional. (*He starts to laugh*)

The other two, through sheer nerves, begin to laugh too

She's not dead is she?
Alice Dead? Good Lord no.
Tom She always looks like this.
Alice She's just been feeling a little under the weather lately.
Tom Yes. Too much brandy ...
Frankie Well, put her on the sofa.

They put Auntie down on the settee

It's too damp and foggy for a walk.
Alice Yes. You're quite right.
Frankie (*to Alice*) Who are you?
Alice I'm Alice. I'm getting married to Tom. (*She points to Tom*)
Frankie Congratulations. I'm Frankie. (*He extends his hand*)
Alice Yes. I thought you might be.

They shake hands. He nearly breaks hers. She reels back in pain

Frankie Now I expect he's told you why I'm here.
Alice He mentioned something or other. Yes.
Frankie To put it frankly ...
Tom (*laughing*) Oh very good. Very funny.
Frankie (*grunting*) What?
Tom Putting it frankly. You being called Frankie and putting it frankly.
Frankie (*doesn't understand the joke*) Eh?
Alice Shut up, Tom.
Tom Sorry I spoke. Please carry on.
Frankie As I was saying, I've come for the cash.
Alice (*quickly*) We haven't got any cash.
Frankie I'd like to believe that, Alice. I really would.
Tom It's true.
Alice There is no money.
Frankie (*pointing at Tom*) He told us on the phone that he had it.
Tom I didn't!
Alice (*to Frankie*) That wasn't Tom. It was Barney.
Auntie (*waking up*) Barney? Did someone mention Barney?
Tom (*to Frankie*) It was Barney on the phone.
Auntie (*puzzled*) He's very clever, isn't he? I knew a Japanese parrot that could talk once. Pletty Plolly, it used to say.
Tom (*to Auntie*) Oh shut up!!

Tom picks up a bottle of port from the drinks cabinet, opens it and waves it in front of Auntie

Auntie stands up and follows the aroma of the bottle into the 2nd bedroom

Once she is in the room, Tom slams the door

Nutter! Total nutter!
Frankie So? Who's this Barney then?

During the following conversation, Frankie's head moves back and forth from Tom to Alice. Rather like a tennis spectator

Tom He's my brother——
Alice —who robbed the bank.
Tom It was my idea I'm afraid——
Alice —but then he took all our *money* ...
Tom Only it wasn't really our money as such——
Alice —but we were looking after it.
Tom He then stole our airline tickets——

Alice —and buggered off with——

Tom Muriel, who's normally a telephone operator——

Alice —but is now a very rich ex-telephone operator!

Tom And you'll never see them again——

Alice —unless you get your boys down to the airport.

Tom And catch them before they board the plane——

Alice —which they'll do——

Tom —as soon as the fog lifts . . .

Frankie Right! That's enough! Stop it! I'm not stupid you know. You can't fool me. I'm not takin' me boys down to the airport, so you can escape with the money.

Alice We don't have the money!

Frankie The money's here somewhere. I intend to find it.

Tom You're wasting your time.

Frankie I've got the place surrounded. You can't go anywhere.

Tom Oh my God!

Alice (*to Frankie*) Search the flat. You won't find anything.

Frankie (*bringing out a gun from his inside pocket*) Perhaps this will persuade you.

Tom (*shaking*) It's a . . . it's a gun!

Frankie That's right. It goes "bang" if Frankie gets upset.

Tom (*to Alice*) We mustn't upset Frankie.

Alice (*to Frankie*) No, we mustn't upset Frankie.

Frankie (*to Tom*) We mustn't upset Frank——(*He realizes*) Hang on, I am Frankie!

Tom (*quickly*) Well don't get upset. Keep calm.

Frankie (*waving the gun*) Just give me the cash.

Alice (*playing for time*) We'd better start looking, Tom.

Tom (*to Alice*) This seems very irregular for the police, I must say.

Alice Pretend to look for the money, Tom. (*She looks under chairs*)

Tom (*to Alice*) There is no money to look for.

Alice I know. But pretend there is. (*She looks under cushions*)

Tom This has gone far enough! I'm not looking for money that isn't there. And I refuse to be held at gunpoint in my own home. (*Bravely to Frankie*) Now look here . . . er . . . F—F—F—Frankie. (*He advances slowly towards Frankie*)

Frankie (*waving the gun*) Yeah?

Alice Don't Tom! He'll kill us.

Tom (*to Frankie*) I don't like your behaviour.

Frankie Is that a fact?

Tom What would the Chief of the local police say if he knew the way you're treating us?

Frankie I don't give a monkey's. Just give me the cash.

Tom (*can't believe this*) You don't give a monkey's? Well you're a fine example.

Frankie He's not going to know, is he? So what does it matter?

Tom Surely he could read the report?

Frankie Report?

Tom All the details.

Frankie (*considering this*) He can read it in the papers if he wants. (*Laughing*) Or watch Police Five.

Tom Read it in the papers? Surely you've got more respect for authority than that?

Frankie (*advancing menacingly on Tom*) I've got no respect for authority at all.

Alice What!

Tom (*advancing bravely on Frankie*) You're one of these rebels are you? Takes the law into his own hands. A bit of a loner? Whatever happened to Dixon of Dock Green!?

Frankie Eh?

Tom You're meant to protect us, not attack us.

Frankie Are you on our list then?

Tom What list?

Frankie Our protection list.

Alice I thought you were meant to protect everyone.

Frankie Only if you paid up.

Tom Paid up?

Frankie If you've paid up we'll protect you.

Alice (*incredulous*) You mean to say you're running a protection racket?

Frankie Me and the boys. Yeah.

Tom I don't believe this! I'm going to take this to the Home Secretary.

Frankie Eh?

The doorbell rings

   (*Quickly, to Alice*) Find out who that is.

Alice (*moving to the front door*) Who's there?

Hendy (*off*) Inspector Hendy, miss. Police.

Alice Oh. (*She opens the door a little*)

Frankie DON'T OPEN THAT DOOR!!!

Alice slams the front door shut in Inspector Hendy's face. He lets out a cry of pain

Alice Don't be silly. It's one of your lot.

Inspector Hendy rings the doorbell and bangs on the door

Frankie Don't be stupid. It's the cops. (*He grabs Tom and holds the gun to his head*)

Alice But you are a cop ... aren't you?

Frankie Are you trying to be funny, lady?

Tom (*terrified*) I don't think he's a policeman, Alice.

Alice (*to Frankie*) Who are you then?

Frankie I'm Frankie. I'm a thug. (*He points the gun at Tom*) Like him.

Tom I'm not a thug.

Frankie You were going to the Convention.

Tom I'm an Elvis fan. It was an Elvis Convention.

Frankie I was talking about the Minders' Protection Convention.

Tom The Minders' Protection Convention?
Frankie Mr Pintocelli sent me over.
Tom Mr Pintocelli?

The doorbell rings again, followed by more knocking

Alice I've *got* to answer the door.
Frankie All right, but get rid of him. One wrong word and I'm going to shoot him. (*He points the gun at Tom*) Come here.

Frankie and Tom exit into the bathroom

Alice Don't do anything rash, Tom. (*She opens the front door*)

Inspector Hendy, wearing full police uniform, enters. He has a strong presence of authority and a no-nonsense stance

Hendy Sorry to trouble you, miss. We've had a report of a man and a woman being arrested at the local airport.
Alice What does it have to do with me, Inspector?
Hendy All in good time, miss. Can I come in?
Alice I suppose so, but I am rather busy.
Hendy It shouldn't take long, miss. (*He looks around the room*) Right, now these two people were caught in the duty-free shop. They were buying some gifts before boarding their plane.
Alice Their plane, Inspector?
Hendy Yes. On route to Miami, Florida.
Alice (*looking out of the window*) The fog has lifted then.
Hendy The man claims he is a Mr Barney Weals.
Alice Barney's my fiancé's brother. Unfortunately for me, he's therefore almost my brother-in-law.
Hendy He was caught trying to change a note for a duty free bottle of Scotch, amongst other things.
Alice Caught changing what?
Hendy A fifty dollar bill, miss.
Alice *One* note. Is that all?
Hendy It was a forgery. Counterfeit. We had no option but to arrest him.
Alice Then why have you come around here?
Hendy This is where he says he got the forged note, miss. I'm afraid I'll have to search the premises.
Alice Inspector, I can assure you there is absolutely no money in this flat. (*Quietly*) I've been searching for it all night.
Hendy I'm sorry, miss. I'll have to satisfy myself on that point.
Alice Please yourself.
Hendy (*moving to the bathroom door*) Right, I'll start with this room.
Alice (*throwing herself in the way*) No, no! You can't go in there.
Hendy Why not?
Alice It's only the bathroom.
Hendy So?
Alice I wouldn't forge notes in a bathroom, would I?
Hendy Possibly. The bath would make for a good disposal of the ink. And

you could hang the notes to dry on the towel rail. Now, if you'll excuse me . . .

Alice (*firmly*) No. I'm sorry, Inspector. You cannot go in there.

Hendy I'm afraid I'll have to insist, miss.

Alice My fiancé's in there.

Hendy Then I'm afraid he'll have to come out.

Alice With another man.

Hendy With another man? What are they doing in there?

Alice (*in a loud voice so Tom and Frankie can hear*) They're . . . er . . . having a bath.

Hendy What!!! Two men having a bath together?

Alice (*louder still*) Yes. They're old friends.

Hendy I should think they are.

Alice They've been doing it for years.

Hendy Have they indeed?

Alice You remember the slogan "Save water, bath with a friend"?

Hendy Using the same water, yes. But one at a time, not two together.

Alice Oh you know what men are like, Inspector.

Hendy (*pushing Alice out of the way*) If you'll excuse me. (*He opens the bathroom door*)

Tom and Frankie, each clad with only a towel around their waist, come out. Frankie still carries his gun hidden under another towel. He prods it into Tom's side

Tom (*effeminately*) Oh look Francis. It's a policeman.

Tom and Frankie link arms

Frankie (*effeminately*) I've always liked a man in uniform. (*To Hendy*) When's your night off, dear?

Hendy It's disgusting! (*He pushes past them and enters the bathroom. Satisfied it is empty, he returns*) Right. Which one of you two p-p-p . . . two is Mr Weals?

Tom }
Frankie } (*together, pointing at each other*)   He is.

Hendy Listen sweethearts, you might share the bathwater, but you cannot both be Mr Weals. (*To Alice*) Will you please identify your fiancé, miss?

Alice (*pointing at Tom*) That's him on the right, Inspector.

Hendy Thank you. (*He takes Alice aside*) I don't want to interfere, miss, but are you sure you'll be happy marrying him? He seems to be a bit of a nancy boy.

Alice I'm a broadminded girl, Inspector.

Hendy Takes all sorts I suppose. (*He faces the two men*) Right you two, my name is . . . (*He looks closely at Frankie*) Haven't I seen you somewhere before?

Frankie Don't think so, dear.

Hendy I never forget a face, mate.

Tom Maybe you saw him down the club?

Hendy And what club would that be, sir?

Tom The Gay Club in the High Street.

Hendy (*horrified*) I don't go to gay clubs!! I'm a police officer.

Alice Maybe you recognize his shoulders, Inspector?

Hendy I'm a happily married man, miss.

Tom Then you don't recognize him?

Hendy (*embarrassed*) He just reminds me of someone else, that's all.

Tom We're all the same without our clothes on, Inspector. (*He gives him a large wink*)

Hendy Yes, and speaking of clothes, would you mind getting dressed please. I have an investigation to make.

Frankie holds Tom's hand as they exit into the bathroom

Alice begins to follow them

Where are you going, miss?

Alice It's my bathtime, Inspector. If you don't have any objection.

She exits into the bathroom

Hendy Blimey! A threesome. At least I know where they all are.

He does a doubletake at himself in the fourth-wall mirror, bending his legs in "evening all" fashion. Then he goes into the 2nd bedroom, but soon comes running out again

I'm sorry, madam! I had no idea that you were in there!

Auntie enters from the 2nd bedroom, a half-empty bottle of port in her hand

Auntie How dare you enter a bedroom without knocking first!

Hendy I'm making a search of the premises. I am a police inspector.

Auntie Indeed. And what exactly did you expect to find?

Hendy Among other things, a printing press. A forged fifty dollar note has been discovered.

Auntie Who was the pulcript?

Hendy Pulcript? You mean culprit. The suspect in question was Barney——

Auntie (*excited*) Barney? You've found Barney?

Hendy Yes, we've——

Auntie Thank goodness! Is he all right?

Hendy (*stiffly*) There is no unnecessary violence used by my men, madam.

Auntie Where did you catch him?

Hendy At the airport.

Auntie He got down there? Extraordinary. And where is he now?

Hendy Safely behind bars, madam.

Auntie Good. You want to be careful though. He might break out.

Hendy Break out?

Auntie He needs space. He needs exercise.

Hendy Does he?

Auntie He doesn't like to be cooped up.

Hendy That's his look-out.

Auntie Or he goes a little crazy.

Hendy Oh yes? Cuckoo? (*He taps his forehead*)

Auntie He's not a cuckoo!

Hendy If you'll excuse me madam, I have a search to carry out. (*He tries to push past her*)

Auntie You look out for Tom Weals, he tried to bribe me.

Hendy Oh yes?

Auntie A nasty bit of work.

Hendy (*bringing out his notebook*) Carry on, madam.

Auntie He doesn't want to marry my niece. He wants to marry Muriel.

Hendy Go on. (*He makes notes*)

Auntie But worse than that, he wants three in a bed on his honeymoon!

Hendy (*raising his eyebrows*) Disgusting!

Auntie What are you going to do about that, eh?

Hendy Don't worry, madam. I've got the three of them in that bathroom. There won't be a honeymoon for quite a while. We in the police don't approve of bigamy. Especially if one of the wives is a man.

Auntie Glad to hear it. And please check your files on "Barmy Barney".

Hendy "Barmy Barney"?

Auntie Tom's brother.

Hendy (*nodding patiently*) We've already got Barney. Down at the airport.

Auntie No. This is another Barney.

Hendy Another Barney?

Auntie They're all called Barney in his family.

Hendy (*incredulous*) Tom's got *two* brothers called "Barney"?

Auntie (*nodding*) Probably. And an Aunt Barney.

Hendy (*very confused*) Aunt Barney?

Auntie Yes. Grandmother wanted a boy.

Hendy Is that a fact?

Auntie Anyway, "Barmy Barney" is the one to look out for.

Hendy (*writing this down*) Barmy Barney . . . how will I recognize him?

Auntie He walks with his head at an angle. (*She demonstrates this*)

Hendy Why?

Auntie (*looking at him like he is mad*) All his screws are loose of course!

Hendy Of course.

Auntie So if you see him, you'll pick him up?

Hendy You leave it to us Madam. (*Casually he searches through the bookshelves. A book falls on to the floor*)

Auntie I intend to. (*She takes a large swig from the port bottle*) Would you like a drink, Sergeant? (*She offers the bottle*)

Hendy I'm an Inspector, madam (*He bends over double to pick up the book from the floor*)

Auntie I do apologize. Would you like a sergeant, Inspector?

Hendy (*straightening up*) Certainly not! (*He puts the book back on the shelf*)

Auntie Never while on duty I suppose.

Hendy I never drink, madam. I'm an abstainer. I've seen the bad effect drinking can have on others. (*He stares at Auntie*)

Auntie Oh, I don't normally do this.

Hendy I see.

Auntie I prefer tea. (*She swigs from the bottle*) But tonight is a special occasion.

Hendy Really?

Auntie Tonight I was intending to give my niece and her fiancé a lovely wedding present.

Hendy I'm sure that's very generous of you. What were you giving them?

Auntie Twenty thousand dollars for their honeymoon. To spend in Florida.

Hendy (*suspiciously*) Twenty thousand dollars? That's a lot of money.

Auntie Not really.

Hendy How would a lady like yourself have twenty thousand dollars to give away? If you don't mind me asking?

Auntie I'm a rich lady. I can afford it. (*She looks on the desk*) Now, where is my money? I'm sure I left it here.

Hendy You've lost your money?

Auntie Mislaid it, Inspector. Only temporary I hope. (*She looks under cushions*)

Hendy What was the cheque in, madam?

Auntie No cheque. It was in fifty dollar notes in a large bag.

Hendy You mean the money was in cash?

Auntie (*still looking for her bag*) Of course. I don't believe in banks. Refuse to open on Sundays. No good to anyone.

Hendy It is very unwise, madam, to carry that much cash about. There are thieves everywhere. You might have been mugged in the street.

Auntie I wasn't though, was I?

Hendy Where's your money then?

Auntie I wonder if it's in the bedroom?

Hendy The bedroom?

Auntie That's where I left the plates.

Hendy (*thinking of forging equipment*) The plates? Now *that's* what I came here to find!

Auntie Had them in the family for years. (*She takes a swig of port*) Come on. (*She moves to the 2nd bedroom door in a lurching, drunken manner*) Walk this way.

Hendy (*rubbing his hands*) After you madam, after you.

For a second he copies the way she walks, then realizes and straightens up to walk in a correct manner. They exit into the 2nd bedroom

The bathroom door opens and Alice followed by Tom and Frankie, now both fully clothed, enter. Frankie still has his gun

Alice (*seeing the empty room*) He's gone.

Tom Thank goodness. I don't like orgies. Two's company, three's a crowd is what I say.

Frankie (*pushing the gun into Tom's back*) Shut up!

Alice Well? What now?

Frankie I'm taking you to meet the Guvner. He has a way of persuading people to give him things.

Tom The first thing I'll give him will be a piece of my mind.

Alice Careful, Tom.

Tom It's disgraceful, the way we've been treated.

Frankie If you had given me the money, I would have been as polite as Prince Charles on Mother's Day.

Alice For once and for all, there is no money!

Frankie You told me this Barney robbed a bank.

Tom He did.

Frankie What did he steal then? The paying-in forms?

Alice He's got the bank money and Mr Pintocelli's money. And now he's with the police at the airport.

Frankie You must think I'm stupid. Now move! (*He waves his gun towards the front door*) You can tell the Guvner your stories.

The 2nd bedroom door opens and Hendy and Auntie enter

The other three freeze

Auntie (*to Hendy*) Where's my money gone?

Hendy (*seeing the others*) OY! Where are you three going then? (*He moves over to face them*)

Tom We are going to …

Alice Go for a walk, weren't we?

Frankie Yes. That's right. A walk.

Hendy A walk? This time of night? Where to?

Frankie		The pub
Tom	(*together*)	The park
Alice		The cinema

Hendy Where?

Frankie		The cinema
Tom	(*together*)	The pub
Alice		The park

Hendy (*shaking his head*) No-one's going anywhere. (*He moves close to Tom*) Until I am completely satisfied.

Tom (*stepping back in alarm*) I beg your pardon.

Hendy I haven't finished with my enquiries yet. Sit down!

The three of them sit down on the settee, Alice on the left, Frankie in the centre and Tom on the right

Auntie (*aside to Hendy*) I think now would be a good time to do it, Inspector.

Hendy Do what?

Auntie To arrest him.

Hendy Arrest who?

Auntie Barney.

Hendy I've already told you. We've got him at the airport.

Auntie No! (*She points at Tom*) "Barmy Barney". The Loose Screwer!

Hendy Oh yes. Leave it to me, madam. (*He paces up and down in front of them*) Now I have some questions and I want some answers.

Tom Of course.

Alice Fire away.

Frankie I'm not sayin' nothin'.

Hendy Are any of you "Barmy"?

Tom Certainly not!

Alice As sane as anyone.

Frankie Flippin' cheek!

Hendy It's just that this lady, (*he points at Auntie*) seems to think that you, sir, (*he points at Tom*) are "Barmy".

Tom I don't think she's got all her wits about her, myself.

Alice Tom! How can you say that?

Tom I'm sorry dear, but she's a bit of a nutcase. You have to admit it.

Alice I'll do no such thing. (*She whispers to Tom*) She's just a bit old, and *very* rich.

Tom I don't care how rich she is.

Alice Tom!

Tom And I don't care how poor we are. I have seen more money today than has passed through my hands in the whole of my life.

Hendy Really, sir? (*He takes out his notebook*)

Tom And I don't like what I've seen.

Alice Careful, Tom. Think what you're saying.

Frankie Don't say nothin' without a lawyer.

Hendy (*to Tom*) Carry on, sir.

Tom I want to make a statement, Inspector. I want to tell you everything.

Hendy That's why I'm here, sir. (*He makes notes*)

Tom (*burbling out*) It's all my fault. I was talking to Barney, my brother, about——

Auntie Liar! Your brother is Tom!

Hendy (*to Auntie*) Quiet! He probably means his other brother Barney.

Auntie (*a little confused*) Oh.

Tom We were talking about what we would do if we could do anything.

Hendy And what did you want to do, sir?

Tom I was rather keen to get a cooking badge actually.

Hendy A cooking badge ... (*He writes this down*) Go on, sir.

Tom Well he suggested or rather I suggested that the best ... (*Sharply to Frankie*) Look, will you stop digging that gun in my back! (*He pushes the gun out of the way*)

Hendy (*alarmed*) Gun!!!

Tom Yes. This thug here ...

Frankie (*leaping up, waving the gun*) Nobody move! Everybody stay where you are. (*He moves to the front door*)

Hendy (*to Frankie*) Who are you?

Alice He's called Frankie.

Hendy (*it clicks*) Pinball Frankie! Of course. Into forgery now are we?

Frankie Keep still or I'll use this! And I'm not joking! (*Using his free hand behind him, he fumbles for the door handle and opens the door*) And don't try to follow me. (*He turns and walks right into ...*)

Barney and Muriel, who are entering with two suitcases (NB these suitcases are identical to the ones with the money, but contain Tom's and Alice's belongings, plus an alarm clock and strips of credit cards)

Who are you?

Hendy (*leaping on Frankie*) Right! You're nicked, Frankie. (*He disarms him with a swift knee in the groin*)

Frankie (*bending in agony*) Aaaaahhhh!!!

Hendy I've got you, mate. (*He whips out a pair of handcuffs and puts them on Frankie's wrists*) We've been after this one for months. (*To Tom*) There could be a reward for you.

Tom I don't want it! Keep it! Have yourselves a ball with it.

Hendy Oh very witty, sir. Policeman's Ball, very good.

Alice Tom! It might be a lot of money.

Tom I don't care how much it is. They can keep it.

Hendy I'll let you know sir, anyway. (*To Frankie*) Right, come on you. You can have your little walk now.

Hendy and Frankie exit through the front door

Tom (*standing up*) Barney! Where the hell have you been?

Barney (*putting cases on the table*) We've been released on bail. It was an awful experience.

Muriel Yeah. Humiliating.

Tom On bail? Who paid that?

Barney Someone called Mr Pintocelli.

Alice } (*together*) Mr Pintocelli!
Tom }

Barney He seemed a nice bloke. He said he was an eccentric who helped out people in distress.

Muriel And we were very distressed.

Barney It was an amazing coincidence. He was on his way to Miami too.

Muriel Told us to look him up when we got over there. Such a friendly bloke. Mind you, it's going to be a few days because we've got this court case. But that shouldn't be any problem because he's fixed us up with a lawyer . . .

Barney Who'll get us off the charge . . .

Muriel And then we'll be off to Miami, Florida.

Tom (*firmly*) You're not going to Miami or anywhere. You've both got a lot of explaining to do. (*To Barney*) Especially you.

Barney Me?

Tom You stole *our* airline tickets for a start.

Barney I'd say that's pretty small fish compared to robbing a bank.

Muriel Yeah.

Tom I robbed a bank?

Barney I know you did. And probably more than once.

Tom *You* robbed the bank.

Barney I know that it was my idea, but it was you who——

Alice Never mind who robbed the bank. Where's the money now?

Muriel In your suitcases. Over there.

Barney I'm just surprised that the police didn't search them at the airport.

Muriel Only because that nice Mr Pintocelli had a word with the customs' official.

Alice Thank God it's safe.

Tom It's all going straight to the police. As evidence. (*He lifts up the telephone*)

Alice ⎫   ⎧ Oh no! (*She replaces the receiver*)
Barney ⎬ (*together*) ⎨ Don't be hasty!
Muriel ⎭   ⎩ We can share it out!

Auntie (*moving to the table*) It's not going anywhere. That money is mine.

Alice (*picking up the case*) We must count it first, Auntie.

Muriel Yeah. Share it around a bit. (*She grabs the case off Alice and puts it on the floor*)

Barney Muriel's right. There's enough for everybody.

Tom (*aghast*) You're all as dishonest as each other!

Alice Wait! What's that? (*She listens intently*)

Tom What's what?

Alice That ticking!

A fast ticking noise is heard

Muriel Ticking?

Barney Ticking?

The ticking gets louder

Auntie Ticking? I can't hear any ticking.

Tom You're as deaf as a post, that's why.

Auntie What?

Muriel It's coming from over there. (*She points at the cases*)

Auntie My dress is in the post? What's he on about?

Barney (*shaking*)   From inside one of the cases.

Tom Oh my God!

Alice It must be a bomb!

Muriel Gordon Bennett!

Barney (*to Muriel*) When you moved the cases. You must have set it off!

Tom Oh no!

Barney Bloody hell!

The ticking is now louder than ever

Tom Run for cover!

They all dive for cover behind the settee and chairs, etc. They crouch down and put their fingers in their ears waiting for the impending explosion. All that is except for Auntie, who is standing in the middle of the room trying to work out what Tom had said to her earlier. The ticking gets faster and louder

Auntie (*to Tom*) What did you mean Barmy Barney, when you said my dress is in the post?

Tom (*popping up his head from behind the settee*) For God's sake woman! Take cover!!! (*He disappears*)

The ticking gets louder and louder

Auntie Tell me what you mean?
Alice (*popping up her head from behind the settee*) Auntie! You'll be killed!!! (*She disappears*)
Auntie Nonsense! It's my money and I want it. (*She approaches the cases*) If you're not going to marry Tom, you can't have it.
Alice (*popping up, a last plea*) Auntie! Don't open the . . .

Muriel squeals, Barney swears and then the ticking stops. There is a deathly quiet. They all flatten themselves on the floor

Auntie It's my money!

Auntie opens one of the cases and pulls out an alarm clock. It goes off in her hand with a loud ringing. Tom runs over and looks into the case

Tom It's *my* case. I set the alarm so we wouldn't miss the Elvis lookalike contest! (*He smiles*) This is a case of "Return to Sender".
Muriel Then where's our money?
Alice You mean *our* money.
Auntie You mean *my* money.
Tom It's all my things. (*He pulls out strips containing hundreds of stolen credit cards*) Good Lord! What's this?
Barney Credit cards. (*He snatches them off Tom*) That'll do nicely mate. (*He puts them in his lower jacket pocket*)
Alice I don't believe it.
Tom It's Mr Pintocelli. He's switched cases with you.
Barney You know Mr Pintocelli?
Alice Not personally. But we do have a few things in common.
Barney He must've wanted us to smuggle credit cards through customs.
Muriel Gordon Bennett! That's why he was so keen to meet us again in Miami.
Barney That means he's got *all* the money.
Tom The five hundred thousand dollars . . .
Alice That was his anyway.
Barney I thought you'd robbed a bank.
Tom I thought you had!
Alice Never mind that. Was there any other money?
Barney Only the twenty thousand dollars that was hers. (*He points at Auntie*)
Alice (*to Barney*) You stole Auntie's money? You little creep!
Auntie It doesn't really matter. The money's counterfeit.
Alice What?
Tom What!
Auntie I've been forging for years, Barmy. My money is worthless.
Tom Then why were you going to give it to us?

Auntie I wasn't going to give it to you. I was going to give it to Tom and Alice to spend on their honeymoon.

Tom (*can't take any more of Auntie's nonsense*) You ask her, Alice.

Alice Why were you going to give me the money, Auntie?

Auntie I've been forging banknotes for years in my attic. I've been giving away large amounts to my relatives for ages. No-one ever found out. But it seems today they have . . .

Barney I can vouch for that.

Muriel Me too.

Auntie I thought I'd try dollars out but my eyesight's not what it was.

Alice Auntie! I can't believe this.

Auntie It's true, my dear. I feel that I should give myself up.

Alice Oh no Auntie, don't do that.

Auntie I'm not going to dear. I just feel I should.

Tom I think you should. Make it a safer world for everyone.

Alice Tom!

Auntie I have no intention whilst there are still criminals like you on the loose.

Alice What are you going to do then?

Auntie I've a headache coming on. I'm going to pick up my plates and my bag and then I'm going home.

Alice ⎫
Tom ⎭ (*together*) Plates?

Auntie My beautiful Spode plates. I left them somewhere.

She exits into the 2nd bedroom

Tom Well, we might as well go down to the airport, Alice. Get on that plane to Miami. (*He closes his case*)

Barney I'm afraid that's gone. Took off about half an hour ago.

Alice Why don't we go somewhere else, Tom.

Tom Like where? (*He picks up his cassette player*)

Alice Oh I don't know. Torquay?

Tom But I'll miss the Elvis Convention.

Alice Did you know Torquay is one of the places that Elvis never visited.

Tom He never went to Peking, but I'm not going there.

Alice We can have a glorious honeymoon in Devon.

Tom What about our wedding in Miami?

Alice We'll get married at next year's do. Be unconventional, Tom.

Tom (*baffled*) Be unconventional at an Elvis Convention?

Alice We'll have the honeymoon first. It's far more exciting.

Tom A honeymoon before the wedding? I thought you were an old-fashioned girl in these things, Alice. (*He puts on his jacket*)

Alice Being old-fashioned is yesterday's news. I want some fun! I want some action! (*She picks up her coat*)

Tom (*keenly*) Torquay it is then. I don't know what we'll find to do there. Unless there's a local Elvis fan club.

Tom moves to the front door. Alice walks behind Barney and pickpockets all the credit cards out of his lower jacket pocket. Nobody notices except the audience

Alice Credit me with some imagination, Tom. (*She puts the cards in her coat pocket*)

Tom holds open the front door for Alice. She pulls his quiff off and throws it on the chair

It never suited you anyway.
Tom Perhaps if I bought some sideburns ...

He turns on his cassette player. They both exit to the Elvis song "All Shook Up"

Barney Well, here we are, Muriel. (*He pours a couple of drinks*)
Muriel Yeah.
Barney We can't go anywhere. We're on bail. That means we'd better stay here.
Muriel Yeah. I suppose so.
Barney Get to know each other.
Muriel (*unsure*) Ummmmm.

Barney offers her a drink. She approaches him with a sexy smile and then, deadpan, walks straight past him to the 1st bedroom door

Barney Muriel? What's the matter?
Muriel I need my sleep, Barney. I'm on shift at eight o'clock. Good-night.

Muriel exits into the 1st bedroom

Barney Gordon Bennett!!!

Auntie, now carrying her plates, comes out of the 2nd bedroom. She moves towards the front door trying not to disturb her oncoming headache

Barney moves across to her

Just before you go Auntie, I was wondering if I could have a quiet word?
Auntie (*suspicious*) What about?
Barney (*moving to the settee*) This forgery caper. I've always wanted to meet an expert. (*He sits down on the settee*)
Auntie (*flattered*) I would hardly call myself an expert. More an enthusiast.
Barney (*patting the empty space beside him*) Please sit down.
Auntie (*sitting down*) Just for a minute then.
Barney How do you cope with all those intricate designs?
Auntie (*forgetting her headache*) Oh that's no problem. You just use the straightforward photographic plate principle. The real knack is getting the paper of just the right density, so that it feels like the real thing.

Barney is spellbound as he takes it all in

Barney Amazing. Carry on Auntie, carry on.

Auntie Well, of course, you've got the problem of cutting the paper. If you're not careful you ... (*She finds herself sitting on something rather uncomfortable*) What's that? (*She looks between her legs*)
Barney My nuts, Auntie. They didn't get used!!

The CURTAIN *falls quickly*

The CURTAIN *calls should be taken to the Elvis Presley song "All Shook Up"*

FURNITURE AND PROPERTY LIST

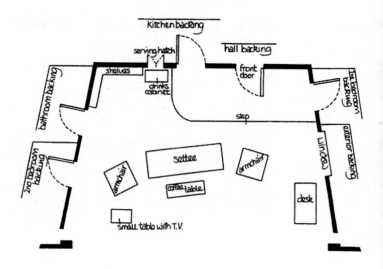

ACT I

On stage: 3-piece suite. *On chairs and settee:* cushions
Coffee table. *On it:* ashtray
Drinks cabinet. *In it:* glasses, bottles of drink including Cinzano, brandy and port
Desk. *On it:* telephone, electrical fan (practical)
Small table. *On it:* old style black and white TV set
Shelves. *On them:* Elvis memorabilia, record player, records, cassettes, books
Carpet. *On it:* 2p coin
Window curtains

Off stage: Keys, portable cassette player (practical) with Elvis tape playing, suitcase containing banknotes, cabin bag **(Tom)**
Suitcase containing banknotes, handbag with brush **(Alice)**
Washing-up brush **(Alice)**
Key, bowl and bag of peanuts in one pocket, candle and holder in other **(Barney)**

Large bag containing banknotes (Auntie)
Tray with two cups of coffee (Muriel)
Auntie's bag (Muriel)
Suitcase containing banknotes (Tom)
Suitcase containing banknotes, handbag with airline tickets (Alice)

Personal: Tom: Elvis hairpiece (required throughout), handkerchief
Alice: wrist-watch
Barney: £3, cigarettes, lighter
Muriel: handbag

ACT II

Set: Elvis tape in cassette player, ready to play "All Shook Up" (for Tom on page 60)

Off stage: Wet towel round hand (Tom)
Empty brandy bottle (Auntie)
Tray with two cups (Tom)
Towels (Tom and Frankie)
Gun (Frankie)
½ empty bottle of port (Auntie)
2 suitcases containing Tom's and Alice's belongings, an alarm clock, strips of credit cards (Barney and Muriel)
2 Spode plates (Auntie)

Personal: Frankie: gun in pocket
Hendy: notebook, pencil, handcuffs

LIGHTING PLOT

Practical fittings required: pendant light
Interior. A sitting-room. The same scene throughout

ACT I Evening

To open: *Black-out*

Cue 1	**Tom** enters and switches on main light	(Page 1)
	Snap on pendant and bring up general interior lighting	
Cue 2	**Tom** switches off main light	(Page 17)
	Snap off pendant and general lighting	
Cue 3	**Barney** switches on main light	(Page 17)
	Snap on pendant and general interior lighting	

ACT II Evening

To open: Pendant on, general interior lighting

No cues

EFFECTS PLOT

ACT I

ACT II

MADE AND PRINTED IN GREAT BRITAIN BY
LATIMER TREND & COMPANY LTD PLYMOUTH
MADE IN ENGLAND